Surrender

FOR GOD'S GLORY

Regina Steward

WestBow
PRESS®
A DIVISION OF THOMAS NELSON
& ZONDERVAN

Unless otherwise noted, Scripture quotations are taken from The HOLY BIBLE, NEW INTERNATIONAL VERSION, NIV copyright 1973, 1978, 1984, 2011 by Biblica, Inc. Used by permission. All rights reserved worldwide. Scripture quotations marked NKJV are taken from the New King James Version. Copyright 1982 by Thomas Nelson. Used by permission. All rights reserved. Scripture quotations marked (NLT) are taken from the Holy Bible, New Living Translation, copyright 1996, 2004, 2007 by Tyndale House Foundation. Used by permission of Tyndale House Publishers, Inc., Carol Stream, Illinois 60188. All rights reserved.

WestBow Press books may be ordered through booksellers or by contacting:

WestBow Press
A Division of Thomas Nelson & Zondervan
1663 Liberty Drive
Bloomington, IN 47403
www.westbowpress.com
1 (866) 928-1240

Because of the dynamic nature of the Internet, any web addresses or links contained in this book may have changed since publication and may no longer be valid. The views expressed in this work are solely those of the author and do not necessarily reflect the views of the publisher, and the publisher hereby disclaims any responsibility for them.

Any people depicted in stock imagery provided by Thinkstock are models, and such images are being used for illustrative purposes only. Certain stock imagery © Thinkstock.

ISBN: 978-1-5127-6222-8 (sc)
ISBN: 978-1-5127-6221-1 (e)

Library of Congress Control Number: 2016918631

Print information available on the last page.

WestBow Press rev. date: 12/28/2016

CONTENTS

Introduction

This is a story of God, who created everything you see and everyone you love. He also created galaxies, planets, and beauty that we haven't even set our eyes on. And right in the midst of all of creation there is a planet, not in the center, not even the biggest, but a planet we call home. And in this place, He created you and me. Each one of us is different. Each one of us has our own story. And when we decide to surrender our lives completely to Jesus, our story of surrender reveals God's glory.

I am excited for you to come along with me as we spend each week following different people in the Bible as they surrendered their lives to God. Each life different, but three things remained the same; God's Sovereignty, the personal choice to surrender, and God receiving much glory through their lives. Week one begins with our need for God and His personal call for us to surrender to Him. In week two we follow the story of Hannah and how God was faithful to her. Week three we follow the story of Daniel, Hananiah, Mishael, and Azariah and how they remained loyal to God, while living and serving in a nation that went against the things of God. Week four we follow Joseph's life of surrender and how his obedience and perseverance saved God's people. Week five we follow Job's and John the Baptist's surrender and how they remained faithful under extreme physical, emotional, and mental pressure. And finally on week six, we see the ultimate surrender of our Lord and Savior, Jesus Christ, who surrendered everything for you and me.

I pray you will give yourself completely over to Jesus and learn from Him and others who surrendered their lives to God. As we journey through each of these stories, we will be able to gain wisdom on how to apply the Word in our own season of life. You and I must be in a daily act of surrender, so we can receive the fullness of what God wants to do in our lives. God wants us to make Jesus our whole life, surrendering our priorities to Him for His glory and purpose. Surrendering our very lives to what Jesus wants for us is no easy task. But as John 15:5 says, "I am the vine; you are the branches. If a man remains in me and I in him, he will bear much fruit; apart from me you can do nothing." Why is surrender so easy to say, but so hard to do? First, because it means we must give up control and second, because we have to give it up continually. Daily, things come our way that hit us unexpectedly and we are unsure how to handle these situations. Our feelings, emotions, and flesh get in the way and the struggle begins between what we are called to do and what we want to do. As I have walked through writing this study, I have found daily I'm hearing God's voice whispering in my spirit, "Surrender this." I also have times that surrender was more difficult because of what the surrender would cost me. Perhaps you've experienced this as I have. It's in these times the surrender becomes almost more than I can stand. Therefore, I have to drop to my knees (and sometimes on my face) and cry out to God, who is able to make sense of things and speak truth to my soul. In that place, He reminds me that He can and will work all things together for my good. But I have to be willing to surrender everything I have been, everything I currently am, and everything I will become in Him.

As we begin to move through this study of surrendering ourselves, let's be reminded to whom we are surrendering. So many times we live in fear or disappointment because the people we trust let us down, therefore, when we think of surrender, we say, "No way, I don't want to get hurt." Or, we believe Satan's lies that tell us God is really holding out on us and everyone else's life is so much better than our own. I know, I have looked at certain people and said, "God is going to do great things in their lives," as if God has chosen some, but not all of us, who are in Christ to be used for His glory and His kingdom. Now I know, and I want you to know, that is a lie from the enemy himself. Some of us have so many negative thoughts in our lives, and we choose to believe these thoughts rather than what God's truth tells us. God wants us to wise up and defeat these thoughts by filling our minds with His truth. We are not surrendering to just anyone. We are surrendering to an all knowing Sovereign God, who surrendered His all for us. Romans 8:32 tells us, "He who did not spare his own Son, but gave him up for us all – how will he not also, along with him, graciously give us all things?" It is time for us to accept God's personal invitation to follow Jesus with complete surrender, fully believing God for an abundant life in Jesus Christ. Thank you for taking this journey with me. I look forward to meeting you on the pages.

Your Sister in Christ,

Regina Steward

In every Bible study, I find a page in the front of the Bible study to write out my current season, including what is going on in my life and where I am at spiritually and emotionally. Nothing long, just a short page of reflection, knowing that the Bible study I am about to begin will meet me on the pages of my life, transforming my thoughts and decisions, making me look more like Christ. I love looking back at what I write on this page at times during the study and at the end to see how life has changed and how much this particular study was perfect for my season on life. Having this written is also such a special reminder of God's faithfulness to have for years to come. So, before you begin, pour out your heart. You won't regret taking the time to reflect where you are in your current season.

Today's Date: _____

WEEK 1

SURRENDER ALL I AM

A Willing Mind

"… acknowledge the God of your father, and serve him with wholehearted devotion and with a willing mind, for the Lord searches every heart and understands every motive behind the thoughts. If you seek him, he will be found by you; but if you forsake him, he will reject you forever." ~ 1 Chronicles 28:9

I am so excited that you've decided to go with God on this journey. Our God is personal. So personal, that He has purposed you to come along with Him at this particular season in your life. He has made you with a divine purpose and you matter to Him. Let's not waste any time. Begin in prayer. Ask God to open the eyes of your heart to understand what He wants to reveal to you today. Be ready and willing to receive what He has for you.

We all love a great love story. Why is that? Because a great love story causes all of our emotions to come alive. Now, this is where you and I can get excited. God has a love story for us. God pursues us like no man has ever been capable of doing. Let's start at the beginning.

Read Genesis 2:16-17

What freedom did God give Adam and Eve? (v. 16)

Why did God say they were not to eat of the tree of knowledge of good and evil? (v. 17)

Why did God give Adam and Eve a choice? Why does God give us a choice?

Read Genesis 3:1-7.

I want you to imagine yourself as Eve for a moment. You are sitting in the garden and hear God coming. Normally, you excitedly run towards the sound of God's voice because you've enjoyed his presence in the garden so many times before, however, on this particular day, Genesis 3:1-7 happens and everything changes!

Take a moment and think about your own life. Can you remember when you first fell in love with Jesus? You were most likely as excited and eager to meet with Him as Eve was to meet with God. It is easy to be excited when we are in complete obedience to God, but way too often the serpent slips into our lives and our own Genesis 3:1-7 begins to unfold. Suddenly we find that our fellowship with God is broken. During these times, we begin to ask ourselves, "What happened and how did I get here"?

2 Corinthians 11:3 says,

"But I am afraid that just as Eve was _____ by the serpent's

cunning, your _____ may somehow be led astray from your

_____ and _____ devotion to Christ."

But I am afraid that just as Eve was deceived by the serpent's cunning, your minds may somehow be led astray from your sincere and pure devotion to Christ.

2 Corinthians 11:3

Name a time you found yourself in a place where you were questioning yourself and your relationship with God.

If you are anything like me, you might have begun to believe the lies the crafty serpent has told you. Or possibly you have begun to question if God is holding out on you? Perhaps you've even looked at others and thought to yourself, "well, everyone else is doing this or everyone else has that and I certainly deserve no less!" Do not be deceived!

What does 1 Peter 5:8 tell us about our enemy?

Please refer back to Genesis 3:1-7 and notice that when Satan attacks, he never points us to the tree of life or to the abundance of trees God has given us to enjoy. No, the enemy points us straight to the one and only tree that God has specifically commanded us to avoid.

Genesis 3:6	1 John 2:15-17
Read Genesis 3:6 and list the three things Eve observed about the fruit.	*Now read 1 John 2:15-17. Look closely at verse 16 and list three things that are not from the Father, but from the world.*
1. _____	1. _____
2. _____	2. _____
3. _____	3. _____

We have to wise up. Satan is not using anything new. He is still targeting the same thing today that he did in the beginning of time. There are over 2000 years difference between these verses in Genesis and 1 John. Isn't it amazing how God used Moses and the apostle Paul to speak the same truth so many years apart?

Cravings

First, let's compare "the fruit was good for food" with "the cravings of sinful man". There are basic needs that we have in the flesh that are good for us. But when we are tempted to crave these things in a sinful way, we are on dangerous ground. What are some things you can think of that might fit into this category?

How can these things become a temptation through the craving of our sinful nature?

Lustful Eyes

Next we see the "lust of the eyes." Is there any person or anything in your life right now that has caught your eye? You find yourself spending a great amount of time, thoughts, and attention, focusing on this person or thing, instead of focusing on the things God wants you to focus on.

Read James 1:14-15 in the margin and fill in the blanks.

But each one is tempted when he is drawn away by his own desires and enticed. Then, when desire has conceived, it gives birth to sin; and sin, when it is full-grown, brings forth death. James 1:14-15

"But each one is _____ when he is _____ away

by his own_____ and _____. Then,

when _____ has _____, it gives _____ to;

_____ and sin, when it is full-grown, _____ forth _____."

Boastful Pride

Now back to 1 John 2:16 for the last one, the boastful pride of life. What am I referring to? The boasting of what one has or does. Often times we find ourselves talking about what "I" have, what "I" am doing, and who "I" know.

Take a look at Jeremiah 9:23-24. What do we learn in these verses?

As we conclude day one, let me remind you that God has placed you in the garden to be free. In Genesis 2:16, God did not give Adam a list of restrictions, but a life of freedom. John 10:10 affirms that the enemy is the one out to destroy us and that Christ came so that we may have abundant life.

What does Galatians 5:1 say?

I think God has made it very clear that He is not holding out on us. Wouldn't you agree?

Take some time to look at what you have written today. It's time that we stop making excuses and ask God to reveal to us areas in which we are giving into the temptations of this world. As God reveals these areas to you, ask Him to remove them from your life. Only then can you be free to run joyfully in the garden.

As you reflect on today's lesson and seek God, place your name in today's scripture.

"_____, acknowledge the God of your father, and serve him with wholehearted devotion and with a willing mind, for the Lord searches every heart and understands every motive behind the thoughts. If you seek him, he will be found by you; but if you forsake him, he will reject you forever." (1 Chronicles 28:9).

Where Are You Hiding?

"If we claim to be without sin, we deceive ourselves and the truth is not in us. If we confess our sins, he is faithful and just and will forgive us our sins and purify us from all unrighteousness." ~ 1 John 1: 8-9

I am thrilled that you are back for day two. Yesterday, we concluded with some very probing questions. God has wasted no time shining His light into our lives. Now where do we go from here? Begin by praying that God will open the eyes of your heart and reveal Himself to you.

Let's go back to the garden and re-visit Genesis chapter 3. Yesterday, we read verses 1-7. Continue today by reading Genesis 3:8-24.

What did Adam and Eve do when they heard God walking in the garden?

What did God ask Adam? (v. 9) _____

What did he say? (v. 10) _____

Why was he afraid? (v. 10) _____

The enemy left them standing naked, feeling guilty and shameful, and looking for a place to hide. As we all do, Adam and Eve tried to meet their own needs by making coverings of fig leaves; but their efforts to deal with their own sin fell short of meeting their real need. Only God could provide the covering they needed.

Why is God the Only One who can provide what we need?

_____

_____

We have become desensitized to sin and sin's consequences in our lives because they seem to be the "new norm" in today's society. But I just have to stop and gasp at the thought of the flood of emotions Adam and Eve must have experienced at that very moment. Adam and Eve were accustomed to living in a perfect world with love, happiness, and wholeness. Suddenly, because of their actions, they were encountering emotions of shame and guilt. What a terrible new experience for them!

Then the man and his wife heard the sound of the LORD God as he was walking in the garden in the cool of the day, and they hid from the LORD God among the trees of the garden.

Genesis 3:8

But the LORD God called to the man, "Where are you?" He answered, I heard you in the garden, and I was afraid because I was naked; so I hid."

Genesis 3:9-10

Where are you hiding?

We see from our scripture, that Adam and Eve hid from God after sinning. Take a moment to list some things in your personal life that you are using to hide yourself. Some of these things can be from Satan (addictions, isolation, sin, etc...), while some things are good in themselves (friends, activities, jobs, etc...), but we use them to distance ourselves from God. Name as few or as many things you feel God is pointing out to you.

Of course, for most of us, if we are in hiding, we are carrying many emotions with us. Circle the emotions one might carry into hiding with them.

Loneliness   Happiness   Anxiety   Love   Anger   Fear
Shamefulness   Bitterness   Jealousy   Wholeness   Guilt

Why do you think this is true?

The emotions we carry with us into hiding are a result of sin. When Adam and Eve sinned they gained the knowledge of good and evil. Sin brought consequences they could not foresee and a need they could not fulfill without God.

What were some of the consequences and emotions Adam and Eve had as a result of their sin?

Just as Adam and Eve were not equipped to meet their own need; neither are we equipped to "cover" our sins and deal with our emotions on our own! Apart from God, we quickly look for things to hide behind. We must allow God to uncover and get to the root of what sends us into hiding; then He will provide the covering for it.

Read Romans 3:23

What does this verse tell us about all people?

Read Romans 6:23

What are the consequences for sin?

Adam and Eve's sin separated them from God. Because God loved Adam and Eve, what did He do for them? Genesis 3:21

God made the first sacrifice by shedding the blood of an animal so Adam and Eve would be covered.

Read John 3:16.

God loves us too. What did God do for us?

Read Ephesians 2:8-9 Can we atone for our sins by being good? Why or why not?

Now read Romans 10:9-10. What does it say we must do?

Just as God breathed Adam's name onto the pages of the Bible, He breathes your name and mine onto the pages of this Bible study and ask; "Where are you?" Are you running free in the garden or are you hiding as Adam did and I have been known to do? I pray you too can hear the sound of the LORD God even now as he comes to find you where you are. Listen, He's calling, "Where are you?" He knows the answer to His question, but He's waiting for you to answer and seek Him for yourself.

Who is covering you?

Praise God! As Christians we are covered by the blood of Jesus Christ Himself! But The Holy Spirit is tugging at me and will not allow me to close today without pausing to ask.... Are you covered? If you try to go through this journey without receiving Jesus first, you have missed the entire point and will leave empty. Knowing Jesus as your Savior is more than walking an aisle and being baptized. It is acknowledging that you are a sinner and believing Jesus is God's son that came to save you from your sins, and receiving His free gift of forgiveness of your sins and asking Him to be Lord over your life. Please don't take this lightly. If you know you are not saved, today is the day for salvation! This is the only way to receive His covering! I'm praying for you and your salvation!

Now it's your turn. Take today's key scripture and fill in the blanks to make it personal to you.

"If _____ claim to be without sin, _____ deceive

_____ and the truth is not in _____. If _____ confess _____ sins, He is faithful

and just and will forgive_____ of _____ sins and purify _____ from all

unrighteousness" (1 John 1:8-9).

Submit to His Will

"Therefore I urge you brothers in view of God's mercy, to offer your bodies as living sacrifices, holy and pleasing to God, this is your spiritual act of worship. Do not conform any longer to the pattern of this world, but be transformed by the renewing of your mind. Then you will be able to test and approve what God's will is his good, pleasing and perfect will." ~ Romans 12:1-2

In yesterday's lesson, we learned some truth that is in sharp contrast with what the enemy wants us to believe. When we cover up a situation because of sin, we are in hiding. But when God covers us, it's for our protection. The enemy is constantly lying to us, telling us God is withholding good things from us. The insight we gain from Eve's story is to listen to God, choose His way of protection, and receive the covering He provides.

Genesis 3 shows us God's perfect order and the importance of it.

Who did Satan go to? (Genesis 3:1)

Who did God address first? (Genesis 3:9)

"God has set up certain authorities in our lives to protect us from the enemy's schemes."

Notice that Satan went to Eve and didn't address Adam who was close by. However, when God came to the garden, He addressed Adam first and then He spoke to Eve. We must not overlook the fact that God has set up certain authorities in our lives to protect us from the enemy's schemes. When we walk out from under that protection, we are on dangerous ground. Eve would have been wise to have looked to Adam and to God for guidance. Satan lies to us and tells us that by submitting to the authorities in our lives something will be taken away. However, God's design actually gives us something we need – His protection.

When we submit, we are doing so under the authority of God. It is important to know the whole counsel of the Word of God, because our submission should never go against the Word of God.

Read the following two scriptures and fill in the blanks.

1 Corinthians 10:31

"Whether you eat or drink or _____ you do, _____ it for the _____ of _____"

James 4:17

"Anyone, then, who _____ the _____ he _____ to do and doesn't do it, _____."

We are giving ourselves in obedience to the Lord when we submit for His glory.

There was good news for Eve. She was in desperate need of covering when she realized she was naked and God Himself made the covering for her and Adam. Of course, this foreshadows God sending Jesus, His One and Only Son, to die for us, so His blood would cover our sin, making it possible for us to step out of hiding and into His great light.

Imagine for a minute that you walk into a large dark room, full of obstacles and you have to guide yourself to the other side. Now imagine that same dark room, but you are given a candle to guide you. Immediate relief comes over you because we both know that one small candle is enough to light the way in front of you. Take a look at the scriptures below to better understand the light of Christ. Let's begin by reading John 8:12 and write what Jesus said below.

Remember the relief you had when you knew you would be given a candle in the dark room. Psalm 119:105 tells us, "Your word is a lamp unto our feet and a light unto our path," giving us the light we need for each step of our life. He also reveals in John 8:12 that he not only provides light for even our smallest decisions, but He is the light of the whole world and when you follow Him, you will no longer be in the dark, but have the light of life.

Did you hear that! When is the last time you felt like you were in the dark about something? Perhaps you believed someone was keeping something from you? It is a lonely and unsettling place to be. Jesus says you no longer have to be in the dark about your life. That's great news! Follow Jesus and have the light of life.

Now, read John 14:6 and fill in what Jesus said below:

I am

The _____   The _____   The _____

and no one comes to the Father except

through _____

I was just talking with a friend yesterday, who had been visiting a woman, with the intent of sharing the gospel with her. The woman told my friend she was saved and baptized, however when my friend asked the lady who God's son was, she replied, "Adam." You may be surprised like I was to hear the woman's response. I was so thankful that God sent my friend to this woman's neighborhood to tell her that there is only One Way to be saved and it is through God's Son, and His name is Jesus. My friend did share John 14:6, "Jesus answered, 'I am the way and the truth and the life. No one comes to the Father except through me.'"

I had a similar experience while in New York City on a mission trip. I was working in a neighborhood full of people of various nationalities and religions. Most would say they were following God; however, many of these would not say they were following Jesus.

What about you? Do you know Jesus is not a way to God, but THE WAY to God. The Only Way, The truth, the Life you so desperately need?

That is great news for us. How do we respond to such a great, loving, and merciful Savior, who will free us from our dark places and bring us into His Wonderful Light to give us life in Him?

Take a look back at our key scripture today; Romans 12:1-2 and fill in the blanks below

Therefore I urge you brothers in view of God's _____, to _____ your bodies as _____ _____, holy and pleasing to God, this is your spiritual act of _____. Do not _____ any longer to the pattern of this world, but be _____ by the _____ of your _____. Then you will be able to test and approve what God's will is, his good, pleasing and perfect will."

This scripture is important for us because as we live it out in obedience, the promise says we will be able to test and approve what God's will is, his good, pleasing, and perfect will. Often we hear someone say, or we say, "I want to know God's will for my life." Here's the avenue that allows us to approach such a wonderful mystery. Let's take a look at the four areas listed in this scripture to better receive these great truths.

Offer your bodies as _____ _____

1. Living Sacrifice

God wants us, our very lives. This Bible study is about following Jesus wherever He takes us. What are you willing to give up to follow Christ?

Do not _____ any longer to the pattern of this world.

11

2. Do Not Conform

The word *conform* means to be pressed in to. It's time to answer the hard question. In what areas of your life are you conforming or feeling "pressed into" the beliefs and practices of the rest of the world?

"But be _____ by the _____ of your _____" (see Romans 12:2)

3. Be transformed

Verse 2 says, "but be transformed by the renewing of your mind" (see Romans 12:2)

When you think of renewing your mind, think of renovating your house. The old must be removed to make room for the new. God wants to remove what has been sitting in your life for way too long and do a new thing.

"Then you will be able to test and _____ what God's _____ is, His good, pleasing and _____ will" (see Romans 12:2)

4. Prove God's Pleasing and Perfect Will

The exciting part for me is the last part of verse 2 where He says, *"so you may prove what is the good, pleasing and perfect will of God" (Romans 12:2).*

I don't know about you, but I want the good, pleasing and perfect will of God in my life.

What areas of your life are beginning to look like the rest of the world around you opposed to the transformation God is showing you in His Word? Be willing to say, "No" to the world and "Yes", to the good, pleasing, and perfect will of God in your life.

An Undivided Heart

"Teach me your way, O LORD, and I will walk in your truth; give me an undivided heart, that I may fear your name. I will praise you, O Lord my God, with all my heart; I will glorify your name forever." ~ Psalm 86:11-12

This morning my heart is so tender toward you fully grasping the lesson for today. Some lessons are learned in a classroom and others are learned by living out this life on earth. Walk with me as we dig into God's Word.

What did Jesus say was the greatest commandment in *Matthew 22:37?*

Jesus replied, "Love the Lord your God with all your heart and with all your soul and with all your mind."

Matthew 22:37,

_____

Proverbs 4:23 says, *"Above all else, guard your _____, for it is the wellspring of life."*

As we develop a relationship with God and learn more about Who He is, we see more clearly that what God is truly after is our heart. He doesn't just want our hearts, He wants our undivided heart!

While praying for today's lesson, God brought three areas to my mind that conflict and divide the heart from His truth. They are self, others, and stuff. Let's take a look at each one.

1. *Ourselves*

   Read Luke 12:16-21 below and underline every time you see the words I, my, I'll.

   16 And he told them this parable: The ground of a certain rich man yielded an abundant harvest.

   17 He thought to himself, 'What shall I do? I have no place to store my crops.'

   18 "Then he said, 'This is what I'll do. I will tear down my barns and build bigger ones, and there I will store my surplus grain. 19 And I'll say to myself, "You have plenty of grain laid up for many years. Take life easy; eat, drink and be merry."'

   20 "But God said to him, 'You fool! This very night your life will be demanded from you. Then who will get what you have prepared for yourself?'

21 "This is how it will be with whoever stores up things for themselves but is not rich toward God."

Who did the man give credit to for his plentiful harvest?

_____

This man was about self-pride and what He had done. What was the outcome? (v. 20)

_____

How do we surrender self? As we grow closer to God and seek Him with our undivided heart, our desires will change and no longer will we want to ride the fence with one foot in our will, and the other in His. I know this is hard, because it requires us to lay down our pride, insecurities, and control. But as we fully trust Him with all of our heart, we will find He is faithful and our focus will no longer be on ourselves but on living for His glory and purpose. It requires us to surrender. Surrendering decisions almost always finds me on my knees in submission to Jesus, but praising Him with hands lifted when I've obeyed!

Now let's read about another man who had power and authority and find out what is said about him. Read Luke 7:1-10

How is this man different than the first?

What did he say to Jesus? (v. 6)

What did Jesus say about him? (v. 9)

Because of this man's faith, what did the men who had gone to get Jesus find when they got back?

_____

The difference in these two men was one man allowed his selfish desires to get in the way of his salvation, while the other man put his faith and trust in the Lord Jesus.

Is there an area of life that you have already planned, and yet you feel God prompting you to give up your own desires in order to obey Him?

2. *Others*

Often others, even the ones closest to us, don't understand our need to follow Jesus with dedication and love. Is there an area in your life where God is calling you to follow him, but you are afraid of what others will say?

Am I now trying to win the approval of men or of God? Or am I trying to please men? If I were still trying to please men, I would not be a servant of Christ.

Galatians 1:10

Read and record what you learn from Galatians 1:10.

As Christians, we cannot please the world and those around us. Rather, we must please God. This means, we have to get past what others may think or say. If God is calling you to follow Him in some area of your life, you won't be happy until your surrender to His leading, regardless of what others may think. Without writing names, ask God if there is anyone in your life that is keeping you from having an un-divided heart. If so, ask God to show you how to surrender **them** to Him so that you may follow him wholeheartedly.

3. *Stuff*

Read and Summarize Matthew 6:19-21

As we move forward, ask God to clearly speak to you through the stories below.

RICH MAN #1

Read Matthew 19:16-22

What did the rich young ruler desire? (v. 16)

What did Jesus say he must give up in order to follow Him? (v. 21)

How did the rich young man go away? (v. 22)

What is your greatest treasure? Riches? Power? Position? People? Things? Other?

How hard would it be for you to walk away from your treasure if Jesus asked you to give it up? Would you surrender? Or would you walk away as the rich man did, sad?

I can't help but wonder how differently things might have been for the rich young ruler if he'd been given the opportunity to speak to the next man we visit in scripture.

RICH MAN #2

This story tells of yet another rich ruler who was unwilling to part with his riches. Only this time, God goes so far as to give us a glimpse of him in hell as the ruler realizes the cost of his decisions.

Read Luke 16:19-31

When this man found himself in hell, how did his focus change?

What was his request? (vs. 27-28)

The rich man finally understood the little worth of what he had on earth and the great treasure of having Jesus, but unfortunately it was too late.

Does this mean if someone is rich they cannot surrender their lives to God and serve Him? No. Remember the example of the Centurion in Luke 7:1-10. He had wealth and power, but it was his faith in God that healed his servant, not his money.

Praise God, it's not too late for us! Go before the throne of the King of king's right now and ask Him, "What things must I surrender to follow you Lord?"

Read 2 Corinthians 5:21 and record what Jesus did for you.

I'm reminded that Jesus gave us the ultimate example when he laid down his life for us at the cross. He left the splendor of heaven to be confined in a body in the humble of circumstances. He was beaten, mocked, and led to an old rugged cross, where He died a cruel death, carrying the weight of our sin, so you and I could be with Him. I cannot help but think about when Jesus was in the garden praying before going to the cross. He was stressed to the point of sweating blood, desiring for the cup to pass from Him if there was any other way. But even so, His heart was one with God, saying in Luke 22:42, "Father, if you are willing, take this cup from me, yet not my will, but yours be done."

Fill in the blanks of today's key scripture and meditate on it as you walk out in obedience what God gave you personally in today's lesson.

"Teach me _____ _____, O LORD, and I will walk in _____ _____;

give me an undivided heart, that I may fear _____ _____. I will praise you, O

Lord my God, with all my heart; I will glorify _____ _____ forever" (Psalm 86:11-12).

All that I Have

"Now to Him who is able to do exceedingly abundantly above all that we ask or think, according to the power that works in us."
~ Ephesians 3:20, NKJV

This week's lessons remind me of those times I've cleaned out a storage unit or a closet. You pull everything out, the good stuff, as well as, the junk that needs to be thrown away and you look at it all sitting there. It takes time and energy to sift through it all, but once its complete, you have such a peace and joy. Week 1 of Surrender seems a lot like this. We have just gone to those areas that need tending to and God has been shining light on each one - not so we will live in condemnation, but so we will be set free to serve Him. It's like cleaning out those closets, it's not always easy, but I urge you not to give up! God is up to great things. And when the process is complete, you will be glad you took the journey.

Let's begin today by reading Galatians 6:9 and write in your own words what encouragement this verse gives.

Now, go with me to Exodus 4. Read Exodus 4:1-5 for yourself.

What did God ask Moses? (v. 2)

And what was in Moses' hand? (v. 2)

What did God command Moses to do with it? (v.3)

Verse 3 says Moses did what God told him to do, but when it became a snake, he ran from it. However, what did Moses do when God ask him reach out his hand and take the tail of the snake?
(v. 4)

Moses was a man who loved God and wanted to follow God, but his flesh was just like ours. After one step of obedience, he looked at what was ahead and ran in fear. However, he continued to listen to the Word of God and obeyed. What did Moses do to demonstrate his faith in God in verse 4?

O Lord, I have never been eloquent, neither in the past nor since you have spoken to your servant. I am slow of speech and tongue.

How did God reveal His Sovereign power to Moses?

What did God say His purpose was in having Moses do? (Verse 5)

Now read Exodus 4:6-9

What series of steps did God take Moses through in these verses and why?

Exodus 4:10

God has no problem believing He can do anything He says He can do. The real question; Do you believe He can do what He says He can do? Do you believe He can accomplish His will in your life to bring salvation to many?

God didn't tell Moses this so he would believe, but that others would believe. God was using the process to first build the faith of Moses so he could lead others to believe.

Read verses 10-17

I think this is an interesting conversation Moses has with God after seeing God do such amazing miracles before His eyes. However, I cannot judge, because Moses' conversation looks a lot like me. What did Moses say to God about His weakness?

How did God respond in verse 11?

However, Moses' fear and insecurity caused him to respond by saying what in verse 13?

Here is God Almighty, who just showed Himself miraculous to Moses and Moses responds with, "Send someone else." I cannot tell you how many times I, too, have looked around and thought God must be talking to someone else. Just like Moses, I have concentrated so much on my own weakness and have drowned out the voice telling me, "I will do it through you." However, all the evidence of God's past miracles proves God is able to even use me despite my greatest weaknesses.

Verses 14-17 reveal God was angry, but in His anger He had grace and mercy. I am thankful for God's amazing grace and mercy, even when we show such unbelief.

Now let's fast forward and read Matthew 14: 25-32

What did Peter ask Jesus? (v. 28)

What happened to Peter when he took his focus off Jesus, who gave him the ability to walk on the water? (v. 30)

Look back at Exodus 4:10

What did Moses say to God?

Scripture tells us that Moses has just experienced God doing a miracle that was intended specifically for him and he continues to doubt how he could be used by God. Both Moses and Peter showed some faith, but when they were asked to do something out of their comfort zone, they didn't see it was not about their abilities, but Gods. It's so easy to get caught up in the enemy's lies, take our eyes off of God, and focus instead on ourselves, our human ability, and our pride.

Have you found yourself, like Moses, making excuses? What excuses have you given God lately?

Or can you relate to Peter? You had enough courage to get out of the boat, but somewhere along the way, you've started sinking.

I hope you find comfort in knowing that both Moses and Peter, who God used in mighty ways for His kingdom, experienced times of weakness that seemed to overshadow their faith. Like Moses, I too have pointed out all my weaknesses to God and questioned if He wanted to use me in the way He was leading. And I've also been like Peter. Finally, getting the courage to step out of the boat, but then circumstances rise up against me, as the waves did Peter, and think I'm going to drown. It's interesting to me that Peter wasn't sinking from the waves or wind overtaking him. Rather it was the thought of the winds and waves that caused him to weaken in faith.

Read Philippians 4:4-13

Paul, like Moses and Peter, was a man who was called by God and had to take great steps of faith in order to complete the mission God had for him. He reminds us in Philippians 4 that we don't need to be anxious about anything. Instead we need to think on what is true, noble, lovely, just, and of good report. Paul then tells us that he knows what it is like to have much and to be in need. In both situations he knows how to be content.

What did Paul say in verse 13?

Let's look back at Moses.

What did God command Moses to do with his staff? Exodus 4:3

> Rick Warren, pastor of Saddleback Church, made a great point when he described what Moses' staff represented. *The staff represented three things. His identity, income, and influence.*
>
> 1. *It's a symbol of his identity, he was a shepherd.*
> 2. *It's a symbol of his income, because all his assets are tied up in sheep.*
> 3. *It's a symbol of his influence. The staff was used to care for and lead the sheep.*[1]

Let's bring this a little closer to home. It's time for you to think about everything God has entrusted you with. This could be your gifts, abilities, influence, positions, children, stuff, and even your weaknesses and insecurities. List everything that comes to mind.

Now, this is the hard question. Are you willing to give God full access to what He's given you? If God asked you to lay it all down for His glory, what would you say?

Both Moses and Peter were used by God to influence others.

Chris Tomlin has a song "I Will Follow" that is a favorite for me and my family. When our son Elijah was only three, I heard him singing some of the lyrics, "Where you go, I'll go. Where you move, I'll move. I will follow You." I thought back to all of those times we would sing this with our kids especially in the summer before we made our first move from our hometown, away from everyone and everything familiar. After the move, God spoke to me in my spirit and said, "Your faith and the steps you take really will affect your children's faith and the steps they take." I'm so thankful I serve a God who speaks truth and affirmation when we live by faith and step out of the boat!

Now look back at today's key scripture and fill in the blanks.

"Now to _____, who _____ _____, to do exceedingly abundantly above all

that we ask or think, according to _____ power that is at _____ in us" (Ephesians 3:20, NKJV)

Who is able? **<u>HE IS ABLE</u>**!

It takes faith to know and admit that we are not able, but God is able through us. Who would have ever guessed God would have used the staff of a shepherd to perform such miracles and deliver all of God's people. Don't underestimate what God wants to do with what He has given you. There is no place for self-focus. Let go of those things that cause you to doubt and let God be God. You don't have to plan it all out. Just obey today.

Yesterday, we talked about giving up self. Today, it's time to lay down what God has given you and ask Him to use it to do the miraculous. Take time right now in prayer and surrender all you've been given. By faith give God full access to use all of these things in your life for His glory.

Notes

1. *Warren, R. (2006, July). Rick Warren: On a life of purpose. [Video file]. Retrieved from https://www.ted.com/talks/rick_warren_on_a_life_of_purpose/transcipt?language=en.*

WEEK 2

FROM DESPERATION TO DEDICATION

Get Up and Go to God

"In my distress I called to the LORD; I cried to my God for help. From His temple He heard my voice; my cry came before Him, into His ears." ~Psalm 18:6

This week we are going to take a journey back in time and learn about a woman, named Hannah, and her son Samuel who God used in a profound way. As we begin our walk with Hannah, I want us to remember that God's word is alive and active. So whatever season or circumstance you are going through today, pray God gives you a personal word.

Now, let's begin by reading 1 Samuel 1:1-2.

How many wives did Elkanah have?

Use verse 2 as a resource to write a description of each wife in the space below.

Hannah   Peninnah

During Old Testament times, women who could not bear children were often considered failures and an embarrassment to their husbands. Hannah had zero children while Peninnah, the other wife, had many. List all the feelings and thoughts you think Hannah had.

Hannah is living in a house with her husband who loves her. But she is also having to live with his other wife and children while she has none of her own. As we continue to follow the life of Hannah, let's not forget, this is not some made up fable. Hannah is a real woman with real problems just like you and me. As Christians we are not promised lives without distress or trials.

What does Deuteronomy 31:6 say?

Read 1 Samuel 1:4-7 and fill in the blanks below.

1. Elkanah gave portions of meat on the day of sacrifice to _____. (v.4)
2. Elkanah gave a _____ portion to Hannah because he _____ her and the _____ had closed her womb. (v. 5)
3. Hannah's _____ provoked her in order to irritate her. (v.6)
4. What was Hannah's reaction to this? (v.7) _____

Hannah's season was long and hard. She was provoked year after year. Whenever she went up to the house of the LORD, her rival provoked her until she wept and would not eat. I think it is important to point out that we often want to put a name and a face on our rival but according to Ephesians 6:12, who is our struggle with?

Now read 1 Samuel 1:8. What four things did Elkanah ask Hannah?

1. _____

2. _____

3. _____

4. _____

Just like Elkanah, those who care about us may not always understand the depth of our pain, but they sincerely want us to get through it. Likewise, we truly desire for those around us to understand what we are going through and why we are hurting.

What does Proverbs 14:10 say?

We have to remember there is only One who really understands the depths of our grief and bitterness. What does Isaiah 53:3-5 reveal about Jesus?

He is the same one who is able to deliver us.

Read John 11:19-45

Verse 35, says," _____ _____."

What miracle did Jesus perform?

Verse 45 says, "Then many of the Jews who had come to Mary, and had seen the things

Jesus did _____

_____."

Let's return to 1 Samuel. Hannah's heart's desire was to have a child. What is your heart's desire? What do you want Jesus to do for you? After you write it down, place today's date beside it.

What does 1 Samuel 1:9-10 tell us Hannah did next?

The Scripture tells us Hannah arose. What if Hannah looked at you right now and said, "_____(your name), it's time to get up and go to the LORD!" No one understands fully your heart's desire and the bitterness of your soul except God. It is time to rise up and go to God. Take your honest heart with all its bitterness and anguish to Him. He is the All Knowing Master with the perfect plan. He knows that things have to be set in the right order in your life, before you can receive your heart's desire and use it for His glory.

Write down today's key scripture and your own heart's desire. Use this scripture today to cry out to God who hears you.

"In My _____, I _____ to the _____; I cried to my

_____ for _____. From His temple He _____ my voice; and my

_____ came before _____, into His ears." (Psalm 18:6).

Powerful Prayer

"Let us then approach the throne of grace with confidence, so that we may receive mercy and find grace to help us in our time of need." ~ Hebrews 4:16

Today as we dive back into the life of Hannah, let's remember where we left off yesterday with verses 9 and 10. Hannah had stood up and in bitterness of soul, wept much and prayed to the LORD.

What does 1 Samuel 1:11 say Hannah did next?

Hannah was at the end of her rope and was no longer just praying for her heart's desire, but she was willing to surrender it back to the LORD. This was a pivotal moment in Hannah's life. She made a vow and she did not take it lightly. We have to be very careful in making vows before God. God takes it seriously. "When you make a vow to God, do not delay to pay it; for He has no pleasure in fools. Pay what you have vowed – better not to vow than to vow and not pay" (Ecclesiastes 5:4-5, NKJV). Hannah promised God the very thing she was asking of Him. We have to be prepared and willing to dedicate the very thing we long for back to God.

Continue reading 1 Samuel 1:12-16.

What did Eli, the priest, think when he saw Hannah praying? (v.14)

If you've ever experienced the Holy Spirit grasping tightly at your heart and wooing you to step out into the aisle to take a position of prayer at the altar, then you can relate to what Hannah was experiencing. She was in need of a Savior to whom she could pour out her heart. She was desperate, unashamed, and unconcerned with what others might think. Often those around us don't understand, but Scripture tells us that even Eli, the priest himself, did not understand the depths of Hannah's prayer. He misunderstood her prayer, thinking she was drunk. Thankfully, fear of others did not prevent Hannah from taking a position of prayer in the Lord's House.

What did Hannah say to Eli? (v.15)

Hannah's story clearly illustrates that God is asking us to come boldy and without restraint to the throne of God with our desires. Notice what happened in verse 17 after Hannah stepped out boldy in prayer.

What was Eli's reply to Hannah? (v.17)

How do you "go in peace"? Look up Philippians 4:6-7 and fill in the blanks below:

"Be anxious for nothing, but in everything by _____ and

supplication, with thanksgiving, let your requests be _____

_____ to _____; and the _____ of God,

which surpasses all understanding, will guard your hearts and minds through

Christ Jesus" (Philippians 4:6-7, NKJV).

PRAYER WITH THANKSGIVING = PEACE

Be anxious for nothing, but in everything by prayer and supplication, with thanksgiving, let your requests be made known to God; and the peace of God, which surpasses all understanding, will guard your hearts and minds through Christ Jesus.

Philippians 4:6-7

Hannah made her prayer known to God and 1 Samuel 1:18 tells us that she was able to "go in peace".

How does this verse describe Hannah's face?

Even before Hannah received her heart's desire, she was healed. Her face was no longer sad. Her long battle was over and no longer could she be taunted by her enemy. She was granted peace. Sometimes the first answer to our prayers is not what we are praying for, but rather the peace of God in our hearts and minds. I encourage you to seek an altar of prayer in your house and pour out your heart's desire to The One who can empathize with you.

Read Hebrews 4:14-16

Who is our High Priest? (v. 14)

Summarize verse 15.

How should we approach the throne of grace? (v.16)

Why should we approach the throne of grace with confidence?

According to 1 John 5:14-15, what gives us confidence as we pray?

How does Romans 8:26-28 give us hope?

Let's take a look at our key scripture as we end today's lesson. Fill in the blanks below.

"Let us then approach the throne of grace with _____, so that we may _____ mercy and find _____ to _____ us in our time of need" (Hebrews 4:16).

As you bow at the alter, imagine this... Jesus, your very own Great High Priest is making intercessions for you according to the will of God. Even when you don't know what to pray, He does. Now, that should give you some hope and peace!

All In His Time

"He has made everything beautiful in its time…" ~Ecclesiastes 3:11

Let's continue. Read *1 Samuel 1:19-20*

Take a moment and think back to yesterday's lesson. When we said goodbye to Hannah, her face was no longer sad. Today's scripture says that she rose early in the morning and worshipped before the LORD. Let's join her as we rise up and worship our LORD together today!

According to verse 19, what did the Lord do?

In the Old Testament, the word remember, means to act on someone's behalf. The power of worship, especially in our weakest moments, can move mountains. What began as an early morning worship before the LORD, became the day of deliverance for Hannah. Take another look at *verse 20.* What does it say happened?

Praise God. Verse 20 tells us that in the process of time... the promise of God did come. I think you need to hear that again. Say it out loud. **THE PROMISE OF GOD DID COME!**

Matthew 17:20 says, "He replied, 'Because you have so little faith. I tell you the truth, if you have faith as small as a mustard seed, you can say to this mountain, 'Move from here to there,' and it will move. Nothing will be impossible for you.'"

Look with me at 1 Samuel 1:21-23. Notice every mention of the word time. It comes time for her husband, Elkanah, and his entire family to go up to offer the LORD the yearly sacrifice and his vow. But Hannah did not go this time. She had gone every time before. What was different for Hannah this time?

Can you just imagine the tenderness in Hannah's heart as she softly caressed her newborn's face; and while staring in awe at her precious promise, she quietly whispered to Elkanah, "I think I'll just stay here this time." Hannah finally had the promise of God in her arms. You better believe she was going to savor every moment of infancy before having to travel to the house of the Lord to leave him **forever** as *verse 22* points out.

Now read, Ecclesiastes 3:1-11 and fill in the blanks.

"There is a _____ for everything, and a season for every activity under the heavens:

> *a <u>time</u> to be born and a time to die,*
> *a <u>time</u> to plant and a time to uproot,*
> *a <u>time</u> to kill and a time to heal,*
> *a <u>time</u> to tear down and a time to build,*
> *a <u>time</u> to weep and a time to laugh,*
> *a <u>time</u> to mourn and a time to dance,*
> *a <u>time</u> to scatter stones and a time to gather them,*
> *a <u>time</u> to embrace and a time to refrain from embracing,*
> *a <u>time</u> to search and a time to give up,*
> *a <u>time</u> to keep and a time to throw away,*
> *a <u>time</u> to tear and a time to mend,*
> *a <u>time</u> to be silent and a time to speak,*
> *a <u>time</u> to love and a time to hate,*
> *a <u>time</u> for war and a time for peace.*

What do workers gain from their toil? I have seen the burden God has laid on the human race. He has made everything beautiful in its_____. He has also set eternity in the human heart; yet no one can fathom what _____ has done from _____ to _____" (Ecclesiastes 3:1-11)

Remember, you are not alone. We need to realize God has a plan for our lives and our time table is different than His. By seeking and trusting the LORD, we will receive the blessing he has for us.

Ask yourself if there is an invitation you should decline during this season of your life and save it for another time.

This moment in your life will not last forever. Just as spring, summer, fall and winter will come and go, so shall the season you are in currently. You are being called to embrace what you have been given at this very moment in your life. Will you tenderly savor it, as Hannah did? Or will you hesitantly look back and say to the rest of the world, "Wait, let me grab my keys, I think I'll go with you instead."?

Say our key scripture as you fill in the blanks below.

"_____ has made _____ beautiful in its _____." Ecclesiastes 3:11

"_____ mercy and find _____ to _____ us in our time of

_____" (Hebrews 4:16).

There is a <u>time</u> for everything, and a season for every activity under heaven:

Ecclesiastes 3:1

Day 4

The Choice – Choosing to Praise Him

"I will proclaim the name of the LORD. Oh praise the greatness of our God!" ~Deuteronomy 32:3

Today we begin a new season in the life of Hannah as she makes the choice to fulfill her vow to the LORD. Open up your copy of God's Word to 1 Samuel 1 and read verses 24-28.

According to verses 27-28, what choices had Hannah made?

Hannah chose to cry out to the LORD in prayer; she believed God for what He had promised; she was faithful in what He had given her; and praise God, without delay she kept her vow and was willing to move on to the next season.

What about you? Where do you find yourself in this season? Check all that apply:

I am.........

☐ Praying

☐ Complaining

☐ Whining

☐ Stressing

☐ Anxious

☐ Willing to embrace this season

☐ Willing to praise God regardless of the season you are in

☐ Too busy for the current season

☐ Wishing for a different season

☐ Willing to move forward in heart and mind

☐ Believing God   ☐ Unwilling to move forward in heart and mind

☐ Filled with unbelief   ☐ Willing to take action.

☐ Faithful in the current season   ☐ Unwilling to take action.

Take the courage to obey what God is revealing to you and then believe Him for it.

Hannah made the difficult choice of keeping her vow, by delivering her only son Samuel to the temple. As heartbreaking as it had to have been, the last we hear from Hannah, she is giving praise to the LORD!

Read 1 Samuel 2:1-10 to reveal Hannah's prayer of praise to the LORD.

In verse 1, Hannah states her salvation and deliverance is because of the LORD. She said, "My _____ rejoices in the _____" (see 1 Samuel 2:1).

Verse 2 Hannah gives praise to the LORD for who He is. What does she say about God?

How does Hannah describe the LORD?

How does Hannah's description in verse 3 say God is all knowing?

She continues her recognition of God in verses 4-8. What does she say about God in Verse 6

Verse 7

Verse 8

What does God do for the saints? (v. 9)

What happens to God's adversaries? (v. 10)

God's hand began with one mother named Hannah, who was willing to pray, believe, and praise God, despite all that surrounded her. Because of her faithfulness, Hannah received more than her heart's desire.

Read 1 Samuel 2:11

What does it say about Hannah's son?

Read 1 Samuel 2:21

Not only was Hannah's firstborn part of a bigger plan that changed a nation, but 1 Samuel 2:21 tells us that

The LORD visited her and blessed her in what way?

God's love is abundant! We will forever be grateful that Hannah went the distance and was faithful to God. We can take away from her story the promise that we too can be the women of God he has called us to be. Let us continue to pray, believe, be faithful, and continue to praise Him during our season.

Which of these things is the easiest or the most difficult for you?

Take time to write your own prayer of praise and recognition of God for your season below. Rather than staring at your circumstances or what you are sacrificing, point to Who He is. Pour out your heart to The Almighty God, telling him everything you are thankful for and thanking him for how far he has brought you!

As you reflect in prayer, remember today's key scripture, "I will _____ the name of the _____.

Oh _____ the greatness of our _____" (Deuteronomy 32:3)!

The Choice – Will you do what it says?

"Do not merely listen to the word, and so deceive yourselves. Do what it says." ~James 1:22

Yesterday and today's topic is all about choices. Let's move forward and read 1 Samuel 2:11-18 and see what God reveals to us about the results of wrong choices.

As a child, what did Samuel do? (vs. 11 and 18)

What did Eli's sons do? (vs. 12 and 17)

A tragedy occurred right in the midst of this beautiful story of Samuel. He grew up before the LORD in the Lord's house. He lived with a priest named Eli and his two sons. However, verse 12 tells us that Eli's sons were wicked and that they did not know the LORD. How is that possible? How can something that appears so perfect on the outside go so far as to be called wicked on the inside? Eli was a man of God, who served God and His people. But sadly, in doing so, it seems he may have forgotten, pushed aside, or neglected his own family.

Eli's sons were raised in the LORD's house their entire lives and still they did not have a relationship with God. As parents we have to be very careful to not get snagged by Satan's trap in this area. Sometimes it is easy to get so focused on serving the world around us, or even serving in the church, that we forget those whom God has placed "in our season" right now.

I personally just received this lesson afresh the other day in a practical way. I was making a pie for a family in need. Having enough ingredients for two, I decided to make both, being certain God would reveal to me the recipient of the second pie. Later, I asked, "Okay God, to whom should I give this pie? Then suddenly he made it very clear to me, "How about your own family?"

-What does *1Timothy 5:8* say?

> *"If anyone does not provide for his relatives, and especially for his _____*
> *_____, he has denied the faith and is worse than an unbeliever" (1 Timothy 5:8).*

"Worse than an unbeliever?" Those are some harsh words coming from the LORD. Look ahead at 1 Samuel 3:12-14.

In these verses, what did God say about the sin of Eli's family?

I think the Lord means business and we had better take notice of those He has placed in our lives and what He has called us to do during this season! Think about your own life. Where might you be giving to others, while your own family is sitting, waiting, wanting, and needing? This could include, time, energy, ministry, resources, both physical and emotional. Write anything that God brings to mind below.

"Do not merely listen to the word, and so deceive yourselves. Do what it says. Anyone who listens to the Word but does not do what it says is like a man who looks at his face in a mirror and, after looking at himself, goes away and immediately forgets what he looks like. But the man who looks intently into the perfect law that gives freedom, and continues to do this, not forgetting what he has heard, but doing it- he will be blessed in what he does" (James 1:22-25).

Your turn. Pray and ask God, "What are you asking me to do in this season?" Include the scriptures below in your prayer, making them personal to you, and any other scripture that the Lord brings to your mind.

Ephesians 2:10

For we are God's workmanship created in Christ Jesus to do good works, which God prepared in advance for us to do.

Psalm 37:23 NKJV

The steps of a good man are ordered by the LORD, and He delights in his way.

Isaiah 30:21

Whether you turn to the right or to the left, your ears will hear a voice behind you, saying, "This is the way; walk in it."

Write today's date. After you pray, be willing to wait for God to answer you before you make plans. When God answers your prayer, come back and write your response and the date of the response. This exercise will help strengthen your faith and be a testimony of faith to others.

Today's Date: _____

Prayer:

_____

_____

_____

_____

_____

_____

_____

_____

_____

_____

_____

Date Answered: _____

God's responses

_____

_____

Remember today's key scripture:

"Do not merely listen to the Word, and so deceive yourselves. _____ what it _____" (James 1:22).

Week 3

LOYAL TO ONLY ONE

When Divine Providence meets Predetermined Loyalty

"But the plans of the LORD stand firm forever, the purposes of his heart through all generations. ~ Psalm 33:11

I hope you are ready to join me for week 3 as we embark on the life of Daniel. Today's lesson is going to reveal to us God's work of providence as well as Daniel's predetermined choice of loyalty. When we get to see both God's hand and man's obedience, we know it's going to be a great story. Before we begin, pray asking God to reveal to you exactly what it is He wants you to take away from today's lesson. Ask Him to open the eyes of your heart, so you can clearly see where your life fits in this story. Carefully consider what is happening throughout the narrative and notice every detail God is drawing to your attention.

Read Daniel 1:1-6 and summarize what is taking place.

Now from among those of the sons of Judah were Daniel, Hananiah, Mishael, and Azariah. ~Daniel 1:6, NKJV

Let's not forget that Daniel is a real person just like you and me. Imagine for a moment being in Daniel's sandals. What would it be like to be age 14 or 15 in the city of Jerusalem during this time? You've been raised in a noble family of Judah and taught to love God and serve Him with all your heart, soul, mind, and strength. Then, instantly, in a blink of an eye, everything changes. What kind of thoughts would be going through your mind if you were Daniel?

Nebuchadnezzar, King of Babylon came into Jerusalem, the city of God's people and besieged it. Why was Nebuchadnezzar able to besiege Jerusalem? (v. 2)

Where did Nebuchadnezzar take the things of God? (v. 2)

Jeremiah 25 tells the background story of how Jerusalem had allowed sin to come into their lives. Therefore, God allowed the enemy to come in and take the things that belonged to Him. First the Bible mentions that they took some of the articles of the house of God to Babylon and placed them in the treasure house of their god. Next, we read where Nebuchadnezzar goes even farther as to instruct the chief of his court officials to bring to the palace some of the Israelites from the royal family and the nobility.

Look at verse 4 and describe the kind of young men Nebuchadnezzar wanted to bring to Babylon.

According to verses 4-5, what were the king's plans for these young men?

We learn the names of four of these young men who were taken captive in verse 6. What are they?

_____, _____,

_____, _____

In your mind, pause with Daniel for just a moment and take a look at what has just gone on around him. In Jerusalem he had been purposely selected because of his positive qualities. But once he was transported to Babylon, he was given a new name in an effort to change his identity. McArthur Study Bible reveals the meaning behind the birth names of Daniel, Hanahiah, Mishael, and Azariah. However, Nebuchadnezzar used the "brainwashing" process to change their names to honor local gods, rather than support their former religious loyalties. Let's take a look at his effort to change the identities of these young men.

Birth Name	Meaning		Babylonian Name	Meaning
Daniel	God is my judge	⟶	Beltshazzar	Bel Protect the king
Hananiah	The Lord is Gracious	⟶	Shadrach	Command of Aku
Mishael	Who is like the Lord	⟶	Meshach	Who is like Aku
Azariah	The Lord is my help	⟶	Abed-Nego	Servant of Nego

Information on chart taken from John McArthur Study Bible New King James Version. Copyright 1979, 1980, 1982 by Thomas Nelson, Inc. Used by permission. All rights reserved.

I don't know about you, but I cannot help but think of my own four children as I read about the devastation that has just occurred in Daniel's life. Brian and I personally and purposely named each one of them with meaning. The names Alexis, Bryce, Brianna, and Elijah are so precious to me. I'm certain I am not alone in this. What about your name and the names of the people in your family? In the space provided, write the names of your family members and what each name means to you.

Names are important. If God gave you a new name in your life at this time, what would it be?

What do you think Daniel and his friends were thinking when they first learned that their names were being changed?

"Daniel, you will no longer be called Daniel, but Beltshazzar.
"Hananiah, you will no longer be called Hananiah, but Shadrach."
"Mishael, you will no longer be called Mishael, but Meshach."
"Azariah, you will no longer be called Azariah, but Abednego."

One by one, they were given new names to represent foreign gods. Let that rest on you for a minute. Daniel and his friends' lives hit an all-time low. If ever there had been a time in their lives when they questioned God, this would have been it.

Think about your own life. When was the last time you wanted to talk some things over with God? Maybe you hit a low point and you needed some assurance that God's plan for your life is good. Take a minute and write your response.

Hold on! God brings good news! Take a look at Jeremiah 29:1-14 and fill in verse 11 below.

> "For _____ _____ the _____ _____ _____
> for you," declares the LORD, "Plans to prosper you and not to harm you, plans to give you hope and a future" (Jeremiah 29:11).

Now, you tell me that isn't good stuff. *Jeremiah 29:11* is a well known verse that means so much to so many. Maybe you just read it for the first time, or perhaps it has become a life verse for you. But tell me friend,

Whom does this scripture reveal had a plan for the exiles? _____

Yes, God had a plan for the exiles all along. He knew they were going to Babylon. He prophesied it through Jeremiah. And then he revealed His plan in the middle of it.

> *"Then you will call upon me and come and pray to me, and I will listen to you. You will seek me and find me when you seek me with all your heart. I will be found by you," declares the LORD, "and will bring you back from captivity. I will gather you from all the nations and places where I have banished you," declares the LORD, "and will bring you back to the place from which I carried you into exile"* (Jeremiah 29:12-14).

King Nebuchadnezzar had a plan for Daniel and his friends just as the enemy has a plan for us; however, our God has a plan for us that includes a hope and future. Therefore, in our own Babylons, we don't have to fear. Our God is sovereign and all we must do is be obedient daily to His Word and trust Him to take care of the rest.

There are many promises for each of us throughout the Bible. But God shows up in our lives and speaks personal promises over each one of us as we seek Him. But verse 12 says we must call upon Him and pray to Him, seeking Him with all our heart.

Now that we have seen God's Sovereign hand in Daniel's life, let's see how Daniel responds with predetermined loyalty to God alone. Continue by reading, Daniel chapter 1:8-16

We don't get any farther than verse 8 until we read, "But Daniel"... Oh how I hope in your own story, when God testifies of you, He can say, "But [_____](your name) purposed in her heart not to defile herself." Whether young or old, each of us must predetermine what choices we will make before the circumstances ever come to pass. This is important so we will successfully accomplish God's will in that season.

For Example:

Dating: Before dating…predetermine you will not just settle for any man that shows you attention, but insist on waiting for the godly man that will lead you in Christ. Then, plan ahead what steps you will take to ensure purity within that relationship.

Married with or without kids…predetermine to fulfill the calling God has on your life, instead of conforming to the world in which you live.

Kids are grown…predetermine what should your role be? What area will you serve or mentor in, instead of retiring from service.

The above examples are just three of many I could have listed to get your brain juices flowing. Please take the time to list your own in the spaces provided below.

MY CURRENT SEASON | MY PREDETERMINED CHOICES & PLAN

Now, don't be deceived into thinking that just because you make a choice to stand firm ahead of time that things will always be easy. Actually, it's quite the contrary. Most of the time, you will endure trials and persecutions because of the stand you have taken. I bet if you and Daniel were to have a conversation at this point, he would tell you it was far from easy. As a matter of fact, let's do just that. Let's take a walk back in time and imagine Daniel describing what he experienced as the events took place.

"They came in and took me right out of my home. They placed me in line with other young men and examined our outward appearance. When I was chosen, a knot tightened in my stomach and fear raced through my mind. I prayed all the way to Babylon, not knowing what was in store for my friends and me. As soon as we got there, they called us up one by one and asked us for our names. Without making eye contact, I told them mine was Daniel. I heard the man say, "You will no longer be called Daniel. Your name is Belteshazzar." I listened as each of my friends, and many others, stepped up to be given a new identity as well. Soon after, we were escorted to the dining hall where we were told we would eat of all of the king's delicacies. The temptation was strong and many looked at the food with great desire. But everything in me wanted to scream out, "Don't you realize this is not a privilege, but a trap from the enemy? If we sit at the king's table and indulge in the king's food, we are defiling God and compromising His Law." Sadly, many could not resist the temptation, and their hearts' desire shifted towards the temporary satisfaction that King Nebuchadnezzar could offer. I heard the Lord speak to my Spirit, "Do not be afraid Daniel, the Lord your God is with you. I will never leave you or forsake you." Immediately, I pressed back all the fear that I had carried and determined in my heart to be fully committed to the One and Only True King who could strengthen me." I can't explain it, but once I pre-determined in my heart that I would be fully committed to God, He immediately strengthened me. And at that moment, I knew I was going to choose God's way, even if it meant there would be few or none who would go with me.

When unexpected things happen, remember God is sovereign! You can take heart and be confident in knowing that He desires to strengthen you. What does 2 Chronicles 16:9 tell us the LORD is seeking to do?

"For the eyes of the LORD range throughout the earth to _____ those whose hearts are fully committed to Him" (2 Chronicles 16:9).

Daniel, who found himself smack dab in the middle of Babylon, had no way of knowing what the end results of his obedience would bring. We too need to go into every situation confident that God will strengthen our hearts as we fully commit to him.

As we move forward, the Bible tells us that Daniel and his friends were tested for ten days after they took their stand. Whether it is ten days, ten weeks, ten months, or ten years, the testing will come when you take a stand for God. But Praise Him that we can have confidence in knowing that the testing and perseverance will not be in vain.

Read James 1:3-4 and fill in the blanks below.

"because you know that the _____ of your _____ develops _____.

Perseverance _____ finish its work so that you may be

_____ and _____, not lacking anything" (James 1:3-4).

Read Daniel 1:17-21 below.

> 17. To these four young men God gave knowledge and understanding of all kinds of literature and learning. And Daniel could understand visions and dreams of all kinds. 18. At the end of the time set by the king to bring them in, the chief official presented them to Nebuchadnezzar. 19. The king talked with them, and he found none equal to Daniel, Hananiah, Mishael and Azariah; so they entered the king's service. 20. In every matter of wisdom and understanding about which the king questioned them, he found them ten times better than all the magicians and enchanters in his whole kingdom. 21. And Daniel remained there until the first year of King Cyrus.

What did God give to the four young men? (v. 17)

I have listed a few other important things that we can take away from the passage.

1. The king set a specific time to bring them to himself. (v. 18)
2. The king found none equal to Daniel, Hananiah, Mishael, and Azarhiah. (v. 19)
3. The king found them ten times better than even his best. (v. 20)

Here is where it gets good! Daniel, Hananiah, Mishael and Azarhiah persevered with purpose. Remember, James 1:4 told us they had to be complete, mature, and not lacking anything. This could only be accomplished through testing and perseverance. Our faith is also being tested for this very purpose. I need you to know, that no matter where you find yourself, you have not been placed there by accident. God is the author of your life. He knows the circumstances, the trials, the testing, the positioning, and the timing. As women of God we must continue to persevere, and he will provide the knowledge and understanding that only He can use to complete His story. God is Sovereign in your life and willing to fulfill the calling He has for you. However, you will need to predetermine in your heart where your loyalties lie or you may become enticed by your own Babylon and forget why you are there. God wants to see you persevere with purpose, but the question remains… Are you willing?

Be encouraged as you reflect on today's key scripture.

"But the _____ of the LORD _____ firm _____, the

_____ of his heart through all generations" (Psalm 33:11).

Wisdom Delivers

"If anyone lacks wisdom, he should ask God, who gives generously to all without finding fault, and it will be given to him."
~James 1:5

I hope you are still thinking about yesterday's lesson and are continuing to be challenged and changed daily through His Word as I am. As we enter into today's lesson we need to take another look at Daniel 1:17 which says, "*To these four young men God gave knowledge and understanding of all kinds of literature and learning. And Daniel could understand visions and dreams of all kinds*".

Let's head back into the king's court and begin reading *Daniel 2:1-13.*

Right there in verse one the story unfolds. King Nebuchadnezzar had dreams and it says he was so troubled that his sleep left him.

Who did the king call to interpret his dream? (v.2)

_____   _____

_____   _____

Obviously at this point we do not know what the dream was about, but we can gather from the text that it was so troubling he was willing to go to what two extremes?

1. _____

   _____ (v.5)

2. _____

   _____(v.6)

Let's break this down a bit. Nebuchadnezzar was a king who had power and position, but he did not have control over his own dreams, so he had little or no sleep. Can you relate to King Nebuchadnezzar's mind set? Think about your own self and how sleep deprivation can affect the clarity of your mind. Often times, it will bring you to a point of exhaustion where you are so desperate you would do anything for a good night's sleep. He was clearly distraught and I can imagine he was desperately seeking some relief.

Can you sense the panic in his voice? One moment he is ranting that he will cut into pieces the very men from whom he is seeking counsel; yet, in the next breath he is offering gifts, rewards, and great honor to the one who can give him the information he is seeking about his dream. In the king's moment of crisis, the decision was made. Daniel 2:13 says, "So the decree was issued to put the wise men to death, and men were sent to look for Daniel and his friends to put them to death".

Let's go on to read in verse 14 how Daniel responded to Arioch, the commander of the king's guard, when he showed up on Daniel's door step to put him to death. How does it say Daniel spoke to him?

Daniel spoke to him with _____ and _____.

I didn't want us to skip this point. We too need some wisdom and tact in our moments of crisis. We really have the choice to keep our heads while everyone else may be having a coming a part. The fact that Daniel used some wisdom and tact in His response was the avenue that gained him the time needed to go explain the matter to his friends and for them to seek God for the revelation.

Let's just say, there are times in our lives where situations happen and catch us off guard. During these times, our feelings and emotions can cause us to say and do things that we later regret. What does Proverbs 15:1 say? Fill in the blank.

> "A _____ answer turns away wrath, but a _____ word stirs up anger" (Proverbs 15:1).

I have found in times of crisis, I can do well for a while and then lash out. God continually reminds me to pray. Also His Word is teaching me, "You should clothe yourselves instead with the beauty that comes from within, the unfading beauty of a gentle and quiet spirit, which is so precious to God"

(1 Peter 3:4, NLT). I continually ask God to give me a gentle and quiet spirit, to tame my tongue, and put a guard over my mouth.

Daniel very well could have answered out of fear and anger, but doing so could have cost him his very life and the purpose God had for him. As women, in the flesh, we tend to answer with sullen silence or lashing out. But as we continue to surrender and walk by the Spirit, we are less likely to answer according to the flesh (see Galatians 5:16).

Walk by the Spirit, and you will not gratify the desires of the flesh. Galatians 5:16

After learning of the decree, Daniel did not make a rash decision. Instead, "At this, Daniel went to the king and asked for time, so that he might interpret the dream for him" (Daniel 2:16). Read the scripture and underline every action Daniel made.

> "Then Daniel returned to his house and explained the matter to his friends Hananiah, Mishael, and Azariah. He urged them to plead for mercy from the God of heaven concerning this mystery, so that he and his friends might not be executed with the rest

of the wise men of Babylon. During the night the mystery was revealed to Daniel in a vision. Then Daniel praised God of heaven" (Daniel 2:17-19).

Daniel sought godly friends, he asked them to pray and he praised God for the answer. Let's look further at these three actions.

He sought godly friends. (v.17)

This is a good place for you to look back at the beginning of the lesson and compare Daniel's advisors to those of King Nebuchadnezzar. What obvious difference is there between the two?

Verse 17 said Daniel returned home and explained the matter to his friends. Let's point out these are the same friends who had also taken a stand and was granted wisdom, knowledge and understanding by God. This is an important point because in our moment of crisis, we too need to seek friends who have a proven character of godly wisdom. You will know these friends by their own life choices and if their advice comes through prayer and the Word of God.

He sought godly counsel to pray (v.18)

We tend to waste time and energy in unsure times and in times of crisis. First, we spend way too much time talking about the matter to anyone who will agree with our thoughts and feelings. Also, as we continue to talk, we may point fingers at people or circumstance we want to blame. Meanwhile, the clock keeps ticking, counting down to the one moment that will display whether we are women of wisdom or women of foolishness. Are we women seeking a quick answer or women seeking God? Let's see Daniel's response.

What does verse 18 say he and his friends did?

Let's notice that Daniel limited his conversation to telling them about the matter and urging them to seek God for the revelation.

What is your normal first response when crisis comes and you are unsure of what to do?

It is okay to talk to friends, but don't go with hopes of talking out an answer. Instead explain the matter and ask them to plead with the Almighty God for His help and His revelation.

I am so thankful God allowed me the opportunity to experience the perfect example of this so that I may share it with you in today's lesson.

One summer, I met a godly young woman at the camp where my husband worked. She had committed to be on staff for half the summer. She served God wholeheartedly during her time there, but as her departure date approached, she was faced with a decision. Should she leave camp as she originally had planned, or should she stay for the second half of summer? Everyone around her wanted her to stay and she was doing an amazing job. It was obvious she wanted to do God's will. She was in her own personal crisis about the decision. I clearly remember her seeking me out one night and asking me what she should do. I talked to her about James 1:5-8 and Daniel 2:20-23.

I can't tell you how many times God has proven himself faithful to me when I have prayed these very scriptures. I suggest you writing out both of these scripture references on note cards. Keep them close at hand so that you too can pray them back to the Lord in your time of need. As you pray, asking Him for wisdom, He will give it to you generously. He knows what is in the darkness and light dwells with him.

God is the One who has the wisdom we need and He promises us that He will give it to us. But when God gives us the wisdom we ask for, what does James 1:6-8 say we must do?

God promises to give us the wisdom, but it is our responsibility to believe Him and not waver. This is not easy because people, thoughts, emotions, and circumstances will try to change our minds. That's why you have to be the one seeking and listening to God for the answer; so you know for certain that it was from Him and not from man.

I saw the young woman later that week and asked her if God had revealed to her what she was supposed to do? She said she had sought the Lord through His word and He directed her to a passage about a father's wisdom. She said, "My dad is a godly man and he has always been the one to give me advice. After reading the passage, I talked with my dad and he told me that I needed to stick to my original plan to leave camp and pursue my school work." Soon after, she encountered several godly individuals who continued to ask her to stay. She even had one young man from camp tell her he was interested in pursuing her. Talk about being faced with conflicting emotions and wavering thoughts. I reminded her that the scripture in James tells us to believe God, so we don't doubt and be like a wave tossed by the wind.

This story is so tender because I know from the time we first receive God's wisdom on a matter, until the day we see the fruit of our obedience, there is always a time in between that can be filled with doubts, fears, and temptations trying to lead us in a different direction. We constantly have to remind ourselves that our feelings, emotions, and circumstances will change, but God's Word will never change.

<u>The dream was revealed to Daniel and he praised God. (v.19-23)</u>

"During the night the mystery was revealed to Daniel in a vision. Then Daniel praised God of heaven" (Daniel 2:19). Now read Daniel 2:20-23.

Who changes your times and seasons?
Who gives you wisdom, knowledge, and understanding?
Who reveals deep and secret things?
Who knows what's in the darkness?

We have a God who knows. Did you hear that? He knows! "And there is no creature hidden from His sight, but all things are naked and open to the eyes of Him to whom we must give account" (Hebrews 4:13, NKJV).

Let's continue reading Daniel 2 verses 24-28. Who does Daniel say cannot explain the king's mystery?

1) _____   2) _____

3) _____   4) _____

Now fill in the blank below to complete verse 28.

> "But there is a _____ in heaven who reveals secrets, and He has made known to King Nebuchadnezzar what will be in the latter days" (Daniel 2:28).

After Daniel's interpretation of the dream in Daniel 2:24-45, King Nebuchadnezzar could not help but praise God as the One True God. When you and I observe God's great power at work, we must also be very careful to acknowledge His glory to those He has placed in front of us, no matter their positions or status. Even among kings, Daniel was very deliberate in pointing to the only One who was and is able to reveal mysteries.

Now, let's fast forward and sum up today's lesson by reading Daniel 2:46-49 and see King Nebuchadnezzar's reaction to the interpretation.

The king did not just acknowledge God but he fell prostrate before Daniel saying, "Surely, your God is the God of gods and the Lord of kings and a revealer of mysteries, for you were able to reveal this mystery" (Daniel 2:47). We can worship God in any posture, but when you've experienced the Glory of the Lord in the way King Nebuchadnezzar had experienced it, you cannot help but fall prostrate in awe before Him. As we say goodbye today, I urge you to find a place free of distraction to fall face down before King Jesus, and worship Him. As you pray, remember today's key scripture; If anyone lacks wisdom, he should ask God, who gives generously to all without finding fault, and it will be given to him. James 1:5

Invitation to Worship

Jesus answered, "It is written: 'Worship the Lord your God and serve him only."' Luke 4:8

Today we will leave Daniel inside the palace of the king and join his friends, Hananiah, Mishael, and Azariah. I have to admit, until this Bible study, I found myself calling them by their Babylonian names, Shadrach, Meshach, and Abed-Nego. However, I believe their God given names have a divine punch in today's lesson. Come and see for yourself.

Let's take a look at Daniel 2:31-45. In this passage we see King Nebuchadnezzar had a dream of a statue and each part represented a different material, representing different kingdoms. Draw and label the statue mentioned in King Nebuchadnezzar's dream.

As we see above Nebuchadnezzar's dream was a revelation of four kingdoms beginning with the Babylonians as being the head made of gold. Read Daniel 3:1-2. What does Daniel 3:1 say King Nebuchadnezzar took upon himself to do?

Now, why do you think he did this? (Circle all that apply.)

Pride	Fear	Sorrow
Dominance	Humility	Submission

As we continue to look at the life of King Nebuchadnezzar we immediately see that he definitely had a case of self-centeredness and an "all about me" mentality. What clues do these two verses give us to support that theory?

Notice that the same king, who had just bowed down before Daniel and acknowledged the One True God, is now erecting an image of gold in honor of only himself. King Nebuchadnezzar was given a dream of a statue symbolizing many kingdoms. (see Daniel 2:31-43)

Secondly, let's look at the measurements of this idol. The Bible tells us it was 90 feet high by 9 feet wide. As I first read across these measurements I thought to myself, "Wow... that sounds huge." Let's take a pencil to graph paper for a visual of how large this statue was. In the large gray box below draw a statue. (Don't worry about perfection). Now, in the small gray box, draw a man. Compare the two. "WOW... THAT IS HUGE!"

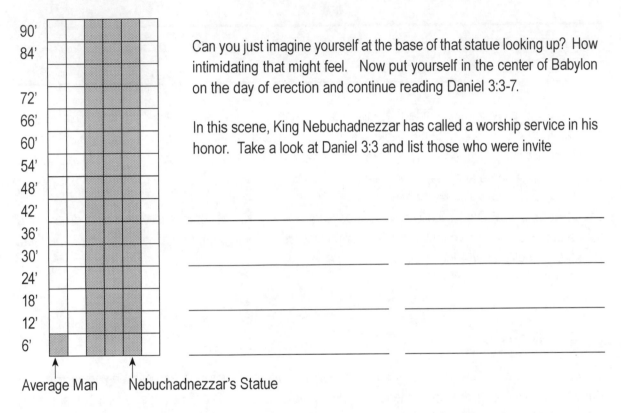

Average Man   Nebuchadnezzar's Statue

Can you just imagine yourself at the base of that statue looking up? How intimidating that might feel. Now put yourself in the center of Babylon on the day of erection and continue reading Daniel 3:3-7.

In this scene, King Nebuchadnezzar has called a worship service in his honor. Take a look at Daniel 3:3 and list those who were invite

_____   _____

_____   _____

_____   _____

_____   _____

That is some gathering! Every leader you could imagine had anxiously gathered around the king at the base of the 90 feet statue of himself to hear the announcement.

What does the Bible say the herald loudly proclaimed? (v.5)

The king had ordered everyone to fall down and worship the image of gold as soon as they heard the instruments begin to play. Let's take a detour here for a moment and discuss God's commandments. So far in the book of Daniel we have experienced two of the Ten Commandments. Beside each name, write out the commandment that each person(s) is dealing with below.

Daniel (Exodus 20:3):

Hannaniah, Mishael, and Azariah (Exodus 20:4):

First, we experienced with Daniel, commandment number one, *"You shall have no other gods before Me" (Exodus 20:3, NKJV)." And now,* in Daniel 3, Hananiah, Mishael, and Azariah are confronted with commandment number two, *"You shall not make for yourself a carved image-any likeness of anything that is in heaven above, or that is in the earth beneath, or that is in the water under the earth" (Exodus 20:4 NKJV).*

As Christ-followers, we have to be careful as we live in the world, not to get caught up in the world's system of following after idols and creating an image for ourselves. We are here to make God's name famous, not our own. Can you think of anywhere in your life where it would be easy to make a name for yourself or create an image?

As we continue reading Daniel 3:8-12 the passages reveal to us that not everyone obeyed the king's orders that day.

How many people does scripture say did not bow down when they heard the music play?

Everyone except Hannaniah, Mishael, and Azariah bowed down. God had been faithful to them in the midst of Babylon as they chose to follow Him. Thankfully they had predetermined in their mind they were not turning their back on God, no matter the consequences.

What were the consequences according to Daniel 3:6?

I imagine their heart raced rapidly in anticipation for the music to start, and then it happened. Everyone, and I do mean everyone, except Hananiah, Mishael and Azariah, hit their face in worship. Please take a visual with me here. Everyone is face down in a prostrate position, most likely in fear themselves of being noticed, and across the horizon are these three lone men still standing. Talk about sticking out like a sore thumb.

Can you think of a time when you yourself were not willing to bow down to a person, circumstance, or thing while everyone around you was?

Let's see how the king responds as we continue reading verses 13-15.

Sparks began to fly. Nebuchadnezzar, in a rage and fury, gave the command to bring the three young men to him. I can imagine everyone had their eyes fixed on them as they were being brought before the king who was furious. At this point though, King Nebuchadnezzar was still so arrogant about himself that he gave them an ultimatum. What were their choices?

First Choice:

Second Choice:

First, the king was mad--really mad. He was raging with fury the Bible tells us. Imagine the three young men as they are in front of an entire nation of leaders and the king has called them by their pagan name. He then gives them the option to bow to his image or be "cast immediately into the midst of a burning fiery furnace." And then he questions their faith and their God by asking, "And who is the god who will deliver you from my hands" (Daniel 3:15, NKJV)?

Is there an area in your life where you might be allowing people or circumstances to question your faith, as the king was questioning theirs?

The young men had to make a choice to stand. We too have to make choices. What's guiding the decisions you are being confronted with?

____Circumstances ____Truth of God's Word ____Fear of Outcome ____What People May Think

Hananiah, Mishael, and Azariah hadn't a clue how this would play out. But they had to make an immediate choice. They did not just decide to refuse to bow, but they chose to use that very platform to point Nebuchadnezzar to their God.

What did they say in Daniel 3:16?

Write Daniel 3:17-18 below

They answered with boldness and faith. One way or another they would receive deliverance that day. Either, God would deliver them from the fire or they would be delivered by the fire into the hands of God.

How could they be so confident that He would rescue them? The same way you and I can be confident. By knowing through His Word what he had already done for others; and then believing he was able to do the same for them. Read Deuteronomy 4:15-24.

What did God warn His people against? (v.15-19, 23-24)

What did God do for His people? (v. 20)

Notice, it was the LORD who took them and brought them out. We too were in need of rescue. Read John 3:16-17 and summarize how God brought us out.

Because of our salvation, we too are called to be part of God's rescue mission. Read Matthew 28:18-20 and describe in your own words how you can be used in God's plan.

As we get back into our story, according to Daniel 3:19-23, King Nebuchadnezzar demanded the furnace to be heated seven times hotter than usual. Hananiah, Mishael, and Azariah were bound in their coats, trousers, turbans, and other garments, and were cast into the midst of the burning fiery furnace. The furnace was so hot that the attending guards were killed by the flames of the fire. The young Hebrew men fell down into the midst of the fiery furnace, but the only thing that was burned was the chords which bound them.

As Christians, we sometimes feel that the fiery trial that awaits us is seven times hotter than usual. These trials are not meant to harm us, but to burn off some things that keep us bound. The trials are also a way of God displaying His glory. Summarize below what 1 Peter 4:12-13 has to say about this.

Let's conclude our scripture reading today in Daniel 3:24-30.

Verse 24 tells us that suddenly King Nebuchadnezzar leaped to his feet. What does he see that amazes him? (v.25)

Let's conclude by being reminded what started as a worship service created by man for man, ended with a worship service created by God for God. Three young men bravely refused to bow down before a man- made idol. Instead they chose to take a bow before the One True God, who is Mighty to save, allowing Him to show His power and His sovereignty to an entire nation of idol worshipers. These same worshippers who bowed down to King Nebuchadnezzar's statue could not help but shift their focus from the king's false idol and recognize the God of Hananiah, Mishael, and Azariah.

John Wesley said, "*Give me one hundred men who fear nothing but sin; and desire nothing but God; and I care not whether they be clergyman or laymen, they alone will shake the gates of hell and set up the kingdom of Heaven upon the earth.*"

These men demonstrated to the world around them today's key scripture. Fill in the blanks below.

Jesus answered, "It is written: '_____the Lord your God and _____ him only"' (Luke 4:8).

No Matter What

"The LORD is near to all who call on him, to all who call on him in truth." Psalm 145:18

This morning, as I write, I'm praying for you. I know the act of surrendering is challenging and stretches us beyond ourselves daily. But please know that you are not the only one walking out this journey. Many women, just like you, are waving their white flags in daily surrender as they walk out their faith and rely on the Lord each step of the way.

At this point we have seen God use Daniel over and over again to interpret the dreams of kings and to help solve their difficult problems. In each case there is a common theme. Daniel sought the Lord for the answer. Today, we will be camping out in Daniel chapter 6. But, let's use the end of Daniel Chapter 5 as a springboard to jump into today's lesson. Read Daniel 5:1-17.

King Belshazzar had a problem he needed the solution for.

Why did he bring Daniel in to solve the problem?

What did he offer Daniel to give the solution?

How did Daniel respond in verse 17?

"Then at Belshazzar's command, Daniel was clothed in purple, a gold chain was placed around his neck, and he was proclaimed the third highest ruler in the kingdom. That very night Belshazzar, king of the Babylonians, was slain, and Darius the Mede took over the kingdom, at the age of sixty-two" (Daniel 5:29-30).

Again, the Bible tells us that Daniel was given power, position, and possessions by the kings of Babylon. But, as we've learned, Daniel did not seek these things. Rather, he sought to be obedient to the Lord; and was placed in the midst of kings to speak God's truth among them.

Moving forward, begin reading Daniel 6:1-4 and state what plans the king had for Daniel? And why? (v. 3)

I am so excited about today's lesson because we are getting to know more about this man Daniel and what made him different from the rest. What set Daniel apart? Verse 3 says he distinguished himself and showed exceptional qualities. I couldn't help but look up the definitions to these words. Take a look at what I found in Merriam Webster's dictionary online. Circle the words that stand out to you.

distinguished (adjective)
"marked by eminence, distinction, or excellence"[1]

exceptional (adjective) 1. "forming an exception: rare 2. better than average: superior <exceptional skill> 3. Deviating from the norm"[2]

Take a look at Daniel 6:3 below and underline what set Daniel apart.

> *"Then this Daniel distinguished himself above the governors and satraps, because an excellent spirit was in him; and the king gave thought to setting him over the whole realm" (Daniel 6:3, NKJV).*

Did you see it? Oh, how I hope it jumped right off the page for you as it did for me when I read it. Daniel had an excellent spirit in him. As Christians, we too have an excellent spirit in us; not because of who we are but because the Holy Spirit of God is living within us.

The king was not alone in making plans for Daniel. The administrators and the satraps had plans of their own. They were determined to find grounds for bringing charges against Daniel in his conduct of government affairs. But no matter how hard they tried, they were unable to find a reason. The second half of Daniel 6:4 gives us three qualities of Daniel's character which explains why they were unable to find a reason. List these three qualities.

Daniel was _____ Daniel was _____ Daniel was _____

How many times have you seen gifted individuals who have been given position, influence and natural abilities to succeed, but because of their lack of integrity, hard work, and trustworthiness they didn't succeed or become all God had made them to be. Gifts and abilities will get you so far, but hard work, integrity and trustworthiness are necessary to becoming excellent in what you do.

A business teacher told our class a story one time about a business owner flying in to meet one of his managers. His plan was to promote the manager in his company. He took the young man out to eat and as they went through the buffet line, the manager hid a one cent pat of butter under his roll. The business owner noticed what the manager had done and said nothing about the promotion during lunch. Later, when asked why he didn't promote the young man he said, "If he is willing to lie over a one cent pat of butter, then what would he do if entrusted to millions of my dollars."

According to Luke 16:10 are the statements below true or false?

TRUE/FALSE   Trustworthy with a few things = trustworthy with many things

Dishonest with a few things = dishonest with much

Whoever can be trusted with very little can also be trusted with much, and whoever is dishonest with very little will also be dishonest with much

Luke 16:10

Some Bible versions use the word faithful and others say whoever can be trusted. God is looking for some women who can be trusted with what they've been given. We all tend to want more of something. More time, territory in our work, influence, or _____ (you fill in the blank). The question is, "can you be trusted with what you have already been given?"

Now, let's move on in our passage of Daniel. Continue by reading Daniel 6:5-9.

After all that conspiring to catch Daniel doing wrong and coming up empty, they realized, the only way they could possibly bring charges against him was to use the law of his God against him. And so they set out to do just that. Let's discuss verses 6 and 7.

How did the administrators and satraps that went to the king appeal to his ego?

According to verse 7, who did the administrators and satraps say agreed with the edict?

_____ Administrators _____ Prefects _____ Satraps _____ Advisers _____ Governors.

The administrators said "All" of them agreed concerning the edict. Let's think about that statement for a moment. Did all of them really agree? How do we know?

We notice a couple of things here. The administrators and satraps told the king that the royal administrators and the others wanted the edict, but we know this is a blatant lie because Daniel was an administrator and he would have never agreed to such a law against his God. We can also determine from these verses that if King Darius had been careful with his decision, he too would have never purposely signed an edict against Daniel because he showed great favor toward him.

Can you think of a decision you have made too hastily and later realized waiting and praying would have saved you and others from being hurt?

Like King Darius, we too must be very careful in our decision making. If made too quickly, we could easily take the enemy up on his offer as he strokes our ego. Meanwhile, we are harming the relationship with the One who is most trusted and loyal. This seems to be a proven tactic for the enemy. A similar instance is found in the book of Esther where a man named Haman stroked the ego of King Ahasuerus (Xerxes) and the king hastily allowed him to issue a decree against the Jews. In the end, however, the intent of the decree was to harm Mordecai, king Ahasuerus (Xerxes) most trusted advisor. In both cases, we clearly see the one thing that caused these kings to forget the effects their decisions would later have on others...their own egos.

Write Proverbs 27:6 below.

When it comes down to it, those leaders who wanted to get rid of Daniel, didn't care about the well-being of the king. Rather, they cared about their own agendas and egos. They only stroked the kings' ego with deceitful kisses in order to gain power and position for themselves. Now ask yourself the following question. Check all that apply.

Am I a woman who:

_____ says nothing
_____ speaks the truth in love
_____ speaks the truth with no love
_____ tells people what they want to hear

As Christian women we don't need to be stroking people's egos. We need to be speaking God's truth. As you do, ask yourself the following;

> ➢ Are we operating under the proper authority (week 1/Day 3); and/or are we the appropriate person to speak the truth?
> ➢ Is it the right timing?
> ➢ Are we genuinely showing love for the people involved?
> ➢ Have we sought the Lord in prayer and His word?

When we apply the above principles, we will come across as someone who genuinely cares about the situation and its outcome, rather than someone who is seeking their own motives.

Read Daniel 6:10 and summarize in your own words what Daniel's response was upon learning of the decree.

Daniel did not panic, but did as he had so many times before. He was disciplined in prayer and he didn't let the law of man keep him from keeping the law of God. Daniel didn't cower down or hide. Instead, we find Daniel, with the window wide open, praying to God just as he had all the times before. You see, his circumstances may have changed, but his God had not. We are seeing daily examples of how Christians are being persecuted all over the world, including our own country for following the law of God. What will you and I do when we come up against our personal battle where the law of the land contradicts the law of God? Will you be willing to follow God, no matter what it costs you?

What is the one thing it mentions Daniel did during His prayer?

a. Daniel asked God to save him from the edict..
b. Daniel doubted the Lord and cried out in despair.
c. Daniel gave thanks to the Lord.

1 Thessalonians tells us, "Rejoice always, pray without ceasing, in everything give thanks; for this is the will of God in Christ Jesus for you" (1Thessalonians 5:16-18, NKJV). And Daniel did just that. *He* prayed and he thanked God. He was wise in knowing God was the only One who could overturn a decree. Daniel had lived through a lot of close encounters with death at this point in his life. His hope was not in man, but in the Almighty God.

Ironically, the very thing the administrators were using to cause Daniel to be put to death is the same thing that would bring Him life and sift out the evil in leadership. Is there a situation or circumstance you feel is causing you to "be put to death"?

Daniel saw that it was necessary to pray throughout the day. Think about your life. In the past week, how much time did you spend in prayer?

The edict issued by the king ordered no one to pray for thirty days. Let's end today with a challenge to commit to do just the opposite. Begin by setting a specific amount of time aside to pray daily. As you pray, I urge you to record in a journal how God answers your prayers and what He reveals to you.

Remember today's key scripture as you pray. The LORD is near to all who call on him, to all who call on him in truth. Psalm 145:18

Commitment to pray to God

"And call upon me in the day of trouble; I will deliver you, and you will honor me." Psalm 50:15

As we begin today's lesson, I'm reminded of what James tells us in the beginning of James 5:13, "Is any one of you in trouble? He should pray..." Yesterday, we ended our lesson with a commitment to prayer. Today, we will see how Daniel's commitment brought about reward.

Now when Daniel learned the decree had been published, he went home to his upstairs room where the windows opened toward Jerusalem. Three times a day he got on his knees and prayed, giving thanks to his God, just as he had done before. Daniel 6:10

Let's pick up where we left off yesterday. A national decree has been issued that no one can pray to any god or person except King Darius for 30 days, or he will be thrown into the Lion's Den.

Begin by reviewing Daniel 6:10-11.

According to verse 10, what did Daniel do after learning about the decree?

Verse 11 reveals what Daniel was asking God for. Underline his petition below (one word).

"Then these men went as a group and found Daniel praying and asking God for help" (Daniel 6:11).

Psalm 121 tells us where our help comes from. Where is that?

Daniel needed help and he knew there was only One who could give him the help he needed. Often times we too need help, and like Daniel, should drop to our knees in confidence, seeking the LORD for our help. Read Ephesians 1:19-22 and answer the following question.

Who has been given power over all things?

God's word clearly states that He has power and dominion over everything. Why then are there times we may not be able to see the power of Christ in our situation?

As Christians, we always have the power available to us through Jesus Christ. However, we must remember to take the truth of God's Word and apply it to our lives. Sun screen is the best analogy that comes to mind. I know that it has the power to protect my skin from sun burns, but it will only work if I squeeze it out of the bottle and apply it to my skin. When we are desperate and our situation seems hopeless, there Is only one who can do the impossible and overturn any decree, any addiction, any _____ (you fill in the blank).

Continue reading Daniel 6:12-15

After reading these verses, I find it interesting that the Bible mentions the men went as a group against Daniel. Why do you think they chose to go to the king as a group?

I wonder how many in the "group" really were against Daniel, or just didn't want to be the "one" singled out as different from the "group." In college, I remember learning a term called groupthink. Take a look at the definition below.

GroupThink: "A pattern of thought characterized by self-deception, forced manufacture of consent and conformity to group values and ethics."3

Have you ever been in a group and found yourself attached to a decision that you would have not made or been a part of if standing alone?

You and I must be cautious in the groups we associate with. Look up Proverbs 13:20 and summarize its meaning in your own words below.

Most of us are involved in groups. This might be a wise group, a foolish group, or a common group. Daniel himself was a part of the king's officials. What made him different within this group?

As you may recall in Daniel chapter 1, Daniel from the very start knew although he didn't have the choice of the group he was placed in, he had the choice to set himself apart, so that he would remain loyal to God. Let's also know we are all part of groups that are common to all of us; teams, work places, schools, etc... Within these groups there may be a mixture of wise and foolish people. Below write out every group you are involved in. Beside the group label it, wise, foolish, or a common group. And in the third column write how the group has affected your walk with Christ in a positive or negative way.

Groups	Wise, Foolish, Common	Positive/Negative Outcomes

Look back at what you have written as you answer the following questions.

1. Do I have a choice to be in this group? Yes or No and why or why not?

2. If you said you have a choice; then ask yourself if it is God's will for you to remain in this group.

3. What steps have you taken to be set apart within each of the groups you listed?

4. What actions prove your answers?

I hope answering these questions give you a better outlook on the groups you are associated with and where you should be within these groups. We have a responsibility as a member of a group to keep our integrity, purity, and loyalty to Jesus.

Now that we looked at our role within a group, let's switch gears and look at what we do when we find ourselves, like Daniel, up against a "foolish" group because of our loyalty to God and His Word. The men pursuing Daniel's life seem to have the upper hand and are seemingly successful in their plan.

Like Daniel, we to at times may find ourselves up against a group who seem strong, loud, determined, and influential. When faced against these "foolish" groups, it can easily cause us to want to retreat in fear, but WHO have we learned has dominion and authority over everything?

Continue reading in Daniel 6:14-16.

What does verse 14 say King Darius did?

I wonder at what point King Darius realized he had been deceived. How long did it take him to realize these men had plotted to get rid of Daniel, a man who had distinguished himself and had exceptional qualities? I wonder how the king felt when he realized that his signature had doomed the man he had chosen to govern the kingdom.

Although we look at this situation through our human eyes, God obviously was setting up the stage to display His glory. As Christians we have the greatest opportunity to witness to those around us when we are faced with trials that only God can solve.

What did King Darius say to Daniel? (v. 16)

Now read Daniel 6:17-18.

According to verse 17, "A stone was brought and placed over the mouth of the den, and the king sealed it with his own signet ring and with the rings of his nobles, so that…

   A. Darius being king could save Daniel's life
   B. Daniel's situation might not be changed
   C. Daniel could run away and save himself

Wait, where is the hope? Where is the power over any situation we spoke about? So, here we have the man of God who asked God for help sealed in the lion's den with hungry lions. King Darius, king over the entire kingdom, made every effort to try to rescue Daniel (v. 14) and now left distraught at home, unable to eat or sleep, and unable to save his friend (v. 18).

Before we look ahead, isn't this a place we find ourselves in times of trouble, backed in a corner, unable to save ourselves, our loved ones, our friends. When we take an honest look at ourselves, many times we look more like Darius, who was unable to eat or sleep, instead of like Daniel, who took God at His word, praying and believing He was able to rescue him.

What should we believe?

   A. No one can help, so no use in praying anymore
   B. The situation is impossible and I've prayed for years
   C. My God is able to do exceedingly, abundantly more than I ask or imagine in Christ Jesus (see Ephesians 3:20), so I will continue to pray, believe, and wait on Him.

We like Darius, want to "fix things" for people. However, many times our best efforts fail because God uses these situations to change lives, bring salvation, and to display His glory.

Pick back up in Daniel 6:19-28

What I love so much in verse 20 is how Darius is now telling it like it is. He is showing some belief too. Before he even sees Daniel, he states that Daniel serves a _____ God.

What happened to the men that accused Daniel? (v. 24)

I bet King Darius didn't think twice when he turned the table on the enemies of Daniel. Remember the warning of the company you keep.

Not only did the sin of these men cost them their lives, but their families' lives as well. "For we know him who said, 'It is mine to avenge; I will repay, and again, 'The Lord will judge his people. It is a dreadful thing to fall into the hands of the living God" (Hebrews 10:30-31).

Summarize the new decree King Darius made. (vs. 26-27)

What statements did Darius make about God? Circle all that apply.

He is the living God	He endures forever	His kingdom will not be destroyed
He rescues and saves	He performs signs and wonders	His dominion will never end

What happened to Daniel? (v. 28)

Let me leave you with the hope that you are not alone in times of trouble. Look back at today's key scripture and fill in the blanks.

"And, _____ on me in the day of _____; I will_____ you, and you will _____ me" (Psalm 50:15).

<u>Notes</u>

1. Merriam Webster's Dictionary online. Retrieved May 26, 2016, from http://www.merriam- webster com/dictionary/citation.
2. Ibid.
3. Ibid.

Week 4

PRESSING ON

What are you willing to do?

"Therefore, to him who knows to do good and does not do it, to him it is sin." ~ James 4:17, NKJV

It's hard to think that God is present and active when our lives hit bottom. I cannot help but think back to the previous people in the Bible whose life stories we've had the opportunity to share. Each of them experienced very low points in their lives. Today we travel to Canaan to walk alongside a young man named Joseph. Begin today's lesson by praying for God to meet personally with you as He brings His Word to life for you.

Read Genesis 37:1-11 and answer the following questions:

How old was Joseph? (v.2)

What did Joseph's father, Jacob, give him (v.3)

Why did he give him a beautiful coat? (v.3)

How did this make the brothers feel? (v.4)

The hatred did not stop there. Verse 11 tells us they were also _____ of him (see Genesis 3:11).

Summarize in your own words what Joseph did that added fuel to the already burning flame? (vs. 5-8)

Like Joseph's brothers, we too will have times when a jealous root springs up in our garden. A true gardener knows the necessity of pulling weeds. As Christians, we cannot afford to let the bad root grow or it will eventually take over our entire garden. Take a moment to till your heart and ask yourself if there is anyone you can think of that you are jealous of and why you are jealous? There is no need to write it on paper. God knows you and He knows your heart. Just be willing to pray, asking God to show you the source of the root, and for Him to cut it off with His divine sheers.

During this week of homework, we will learn much about Joseph and his brothers. So far the stage has been set for an ugly story of bitterness, jealousy, and anger. Join me as we pull back the curtain and watch God once again prove Himself faithful in the midst of what seems to be one huge mess, all for His glory.

Continue reading Genesis 37:12-14(a).

What did Joseph's father ask him to do?

How did Joseph respond to his father's call in verse 13?

Joseph may have only been 17 when God first revealed his future plans for him in a dream, but he possessed a special quality. He was always ready and willing to listen for his father's voice and then be obedient in doing what was asked of him. What about you? Are you listening for God's voice and ready to obey? What do you hear Him asking you to do?

Maybe you couldn't answer the above question. If not, could it be because you are not able to hear God's voice speaking to you? Or maybe you do hear His voice, but you are refusing to obey what He is telling you to do. Before moving any further in our Bible study it is very important you ask yourself the following question.

Do you hear God speaking to you?
YES or NO

If you hear Him speaking then are you willing to obey?

_____
_____
_____
_____
_____

What is preventing you from hearing His voice?

_____
_____
_____
_____
_____

Read Luke 6:47-49 and describe in your own words what God has to say about those who hear His voice.

Our complete surrender and obedience starts with discernment, the act of hearing His voice and understanding what He is asking us to do.

_____
_____
_____
_____
_____
_____

I don't know about you but verse 49 grabs my attention. In almost every instance of my life, when I felt like my house was literally falling down around me, I can look back and see where God was speaking to me but I wasn't listening.

I much prefer to see my life for the Lord play out like that of King Solomon's. Read 1 Kings 3:9-14.

"Let the wise listen and add to their learning, and let the discerning get guidance" (Proverbs 1:5).

What do the wise do? _____

What do the discerning get? _____

How do we get it? _(Proverbs 18:15(b))_

_____

Read 1 Kings 3:9-14

What did King Solomon ask God for? (v.9)

_____

Did God give him what he asked?(v.12)
YES/NO

_____

Why or Why Not? (v.10)

_____

God makes it very clear in 1 Kings 3:14. "So if you walk in My ways, to keep My statutes and My commandments, as your father David walked, then I will lengthen your days." What does verse 13 say God also gave King Solomon?

_____

If we seek Him with the right heart, desiring to obey him he will give us more than we even ask for.

Continue reading Genesis 37:14(b)-20.

What did the brothers call Joseph? (v.19)

___ R ___ ___ A ___ ___ E ___ ___

Why do you think they called him this?

The brothers had become so wrapped up in their own hatred and jealousy that they could no longer see Joseph for the person he was. Rather than calling him by his name, they nick named him "dreamer", mocking the very way God had spoken to him. I cannot emphasize enough how very careful we must be when we begin having negative thoughts towards someone. The enemy will take every opportunity to use our negativity to cause strife between them and us. If he can, he will convince us to mock them, make fun of them, call them names, or sometimes even worse. Satan will take us as far as we are willing to go. Let's end by taking a look at just how far Joseph's brothers were willing to go. According to verse 20, how far was that?

Today's lesson has been shorter than days past. Let's take that as a cue from God to use our extra time to meet with him in quiet time. Ask Him the hard questions. Is there a jealous root? Are you listening for His voice? Do you obey what you hear?

Remember, there is a willing heart and mind within each of us. Joseph was willing to obey his father and the brothers were willing to kill Joseph. What are you willing to do? Remember our key scripture by filling in your name in the blanks below.

Close by surrendering your will to God as you seek His will in prayer.

"Therefore, to _____ who knows to do good and does not do it, to _____ it is

Sin" (James 4:17, NKJV).

Guilty by Association

"Do not be misled: "Bad company corrupts good character." Come back to your senses as you ought, and stop sinning; for there are some who are ignorant of God–I say this to your shame." ~1 Corinthians 15:33-34

Welcome back. Begin today's lesson in prayer, asking God to speak directly to your heart as you open His Word and read Psalms 1:1. Draw a line to each warning God gives us as it is written in the verse below.

Blessed is the man who does not . . .

WALK	IN THE WAY OF SINNERS
STAND	IN THE SEAT OF MOCKERS
SIT	IN THE COUNSEL OF THE WICKED

Psalm 1:1 paints a perfect picture of how sin can start small, but if left unattended, how quickly it can also get out of control. Let's look closely at the life of Joseph's brother, Reuben, as we discuss the steps of progression that Psalm 1:1 warns us against.

1. Do not walk in the counsel of the wicked.

Can you recall what Reuben and his brothers were doing in Genesis 37:12?

And where does verse 12 tell us they were grazing their flocks?

Take a look at Genesis 37:17 (below) and circle the action words that lead us to believe they were traveling or "walking".

"They have *moved* on from here, the man answered. "I heard them say, "*Let's go* to Dothan"

I am certain Rueben's morning probably began like many before, walking alongside his brothers from town to town and field to field while feeding their flocks. Though he did not expect the day to end as it did, don't you believe he had lived with his brothers long enough to know the wickedness of their hearts and the things they were capable of? Still, knowing all these things, Reuben chose to walk

71

the path alongside them. I'm quite sure he probably thought as many of us, "Just because they are saying and doing evil things, doesn't mean I am." Let me be very clear when I say every instruction from God is for our own benefit. When He warns us "do not walk with the counsel of the wicked" it is because He knows our flesh and what it is capable of. He knows the enemy is lying in wait to use the path of sinners to lead us to places we would not have chosen to go on our own. As Christians, we are on dangerous ground when we continue to walk with sinners, rather than choosing to walk away.

Do you know people in your life you may be dangerously walking alongside of? If so, ask God to give you the strength to walk away. If you do not walk away from the path of the wicked, it will nearly always lead you to the next step.

a.   <u>Do not stand in the way of sinners.</u>

Refresh your memory by reading Genesis 37:19-20 and imagine with me how the scene may have looked.

The brothers are in the field at Dothan, possibly feeding their flocks, eating lunch, or resting, when one brother notices Joseph coming in the distance and brings it to the attention of the others. They all stop what they are doing, and turn to face the horizon to see Joseph across the field. As they are "standing" and watching, one brother mumbles under his breath, "Here comes that dreamer!" Those words were all it took to spark the flame that spread like wildfire among the brothers. Soon they were all speaking in anger and calling him a dreamer. Out of that moment arose the opportunity Satan had been waiting for. The brothers stood together in the field that day, plotting to kill Joseph and throw his body in the cistern, as they watched him grow near. As I've read the end of the story, I can't imagine what was going through Reuben's mind as he stood in the presence of sinners.

Continue reading verses 21-22 and answer the following questions.

What did Reuben try to do? (v.21)

Did he want to kill him? ☐ YES ☐ NO

What alternate plan did Reuben suggest instead? (v.22a)

What did he plan to later do? (v.22b)

What event in verses 23-28 caused Reuben's plan to fail?

Reuben obviously did not have the same wicked heart toward Joseph as his brothers. He even attempted to somewhat do the right thing. However; he still found himself standing among the wrong crowd and found it difficult to make the right choice no matter how right his heart seemed to be. Isn't that so easy to do?

The Bible doesn't tell us where Reuben was at the time the brothers sold Joseph into slavery, but it does tell us his reaction when he found Joseph missing from the cistern. What heart wrenching question did Reuben ask his brothers in the last sentence of verse 30?

Perhaps, like Reuben, you have found yourself in a similar situation, standing with sinners, and are desperately asking the question, "Where can I turn now?" I come to tell you that all is not lost and you have hope! You can turn back to Jesus and follow Him, but you have to make the choice. The Bible paints a beautiful picture of this promise in the story of the prodigal son. Read Luke 15:11-24.

1.   What did the son do when he came to his senses?

2.   How did the father respond?

> Both Reuben and the prodigal son found themselves in sin. One continued to hide the sin, while the other chose to confess it. But you must know that the Father was compassionately watching and waiting for both of them to return. Often times we get caught up in the enemies lie that we have sinned too much to turn back. Please know, Jesus died on the cross so you and I could be forgiven of our sins. No matter where you find yourself, the Lord is always waiting with open arms.

> Read and summarize in your own words what Romans 4:7-8 says.

> Let's look at the final step of progression in Psalm 1:1.

b.   <u>Do not sit in the seat of mockers.</u>

Sometimes we just have to get up and get out or we wind up sitting in the sinner's seat all on our own. We no longer resemble who we once were because we have now become one of them.

Continue Reading Genesis 37:31-36

How did the brothers deceive Joseph's father?

Did Reuben go to his father with the truth?

Joseph's story is a reminder that we really are affected by those with whom we associate. Reuben never intended to sell Joseph into slavery or lie to his father, but take note of what he was guilty of as you fill in the blanks below.

Reuben _____ in the counsel of the wicked as he and his brothers fed their flocks.

Reuben _____ in the way of sinners as his brothers called Joseph a dreamer and plotted to kill him.

Reuben _____ in the seat of mockers as he went along with the lie his brothers told their father.

We may think, O I am just flirting with sin, how does that hurt anyone? I'm not planning on doing anything, just walking with them, or hanging out. That is a lie from the enemy to think something minor cannot become something major. It always starts with a thought and the thought if not captured will be entertained and will set itself up as a stronghold. Before you know it, a pattern of thinking begins and then we talk about it. Eventually our actions are set in motion. In Reuben's case, when all was said and done, he was the one sitting in the mocker's seat, playing with sin when he chose to continue in the lie his brothers were hiding.

You too may have never intended on sitting in this seat, but before you realized it, you are. Like Reuben, you really do have a choice to get up and get out. Say that out loud, "I really do have the choice to GET UP and GET OUT."

Read Psalm 1:1-3. Verses 1 and 2 describe what Christians should do. We've already looked at verse 1. In verse 2, what does a Christian do to be blessed?

Verse 3 describes a Christian like a tree with a continuous supply of water. Read John 4:13-14. According to this scripture, who is the living water?

By separating ourselves from sin and reading and meditating on God's Word, we demonstrate the qualities of a strong and healthy fruit tree with a never ending supply of the living water that comes from Christ Jesus. Only then can we be a witness to the sinner and produce much fruit.

Meditate on Psalm 1:1-3, draw a picture or describe in your own words what these verses mean to you.

As we close today, I find it so exciting to share with you the similar wording I noticed between our key scripture, and Luke 15:17. "When he **came to his senses**, he said, 'How many of my father's hired men have food to spare, and here I am starving to death" (Luke 15:17).

Fill in the blank below and share in my excitement as God reveals His wonderful Word to us.

"Do not be misled: "Bad company corrupts good character." _____ _____ _____

_____ _____ as you ought, and stop sinning; for there are some who are

ignorant of God—I say this to your shame." 1 Corinthians 15:33-34

Perseverance Through Temptation

"For we do not have a high priest who is unable to sympathize with our weaknesses, but we have one who has been tempted in every way, just as we are – yet was without sin." ~ Hebrews 4:15

This morning my daughter, Alexis, went to the church for a youth workout session. A volunteer offered to train with the students in the summer, so they would be ready for sports in the fall. She told me about the intense training exercises they've been doing and she walked around sore the rest of the day after one of these sessions. Immediately, I thought about Joseph's life of training, as well as ours. I think of these days of homework as the instructions for the training we daily receive. If we press in and don't give up, we will be thoroughly equipped for every good work when the time comes. Today, we are going to discuss an area we all need rigorous training in, so when the real struggle comes, we can take victory over it - **Temptation**.

Think back to the last time you were tempted? Where were you and did you feel like you were victorious over the temptation? Did you feel shameful for being tempted, or even caught off guard? Today's lesson is on exposing temptation for what it is by shining light on it so we can have victory over it.

Think about Joseph and how he must have felt; hated, betrayed, stripped from his high position and sold into slavery. I'm sure there were moments when it seemed impossible to Joseph that God could use any of that to fulfill His plan for his life. However, God knew exactly what He was doing in every part of Joseph's life and how each part would be used to fulfill God's plan in Joseph's life. Let's go back to Genesis and continue following Joseph. Let's look further into Joseph's life as he arrives in Egypt. Begin reading today in Genesis 39:1-6

Who bought Joseph from the Ishmaelites? (v.1)

   a. Potiphar
   b. an Egyptian, one of Pharaoh's Officials
   c. the captain of the guard
   d. all the above

What feelings do you think Joseph may have had?

I'm quite certain one of the many emotions Joseph was struggling with was most likely loneliness. But according to scripture, who was with him? (v.2)

Often times, we experience feelings of failure when we are lonely. However, because the Lord was with Joseph, he experienced quite the opposite. What was that? (v.2)

Below are verses 2-6 and I want us to look in detail how Joseph, who was bought as a slave, progressed to be in charge of everything his master owned. Paraphrase verses 3, 4, and 5, as I did verses 2 and 6 to see this progression.

Verse 2	The Lord was with Joseph. He prospered and lived in the house of his Egyptian master.
Verse 3	
Verse 4	
Verse 5	
Verse 6	Potiphar left in Joseph's care everything he had. With Joseph in charge he did not concern himself with anything except the food he ate.

Read Proverbs 3:1-4 and explain in your own words

I am amazed at God and his ways. Here is an Egyptian leader and one day he buys what he thinks is another foreign slave to work in his house. But as time progresses, something is vastly different about this young man. Success follows him in everything he does. There is such a noticeable success that Potiphar makes him his attendant and everything Potiphar puts him over is blessed. What I love about Joseph's story at this point is he didn't let the past keep him from being successful in his present. Let's be reminded: Joseph has been betrayed and physically and emotionally hurt by his brothers, taken from his position and from his father, and sold as a slave in a foreign land, not knowing what would happen to him. However, instead of seeing him bitter, we see everything he does prosper and blessing others. God gives Joseph success and not just a little success. God blesses everything that Joseph does. He even blesses Potiphar's household because of Joseph. We are reminded from whose hand the blessing comes. We have to be careful to remember that it is not man, but God who gives such victory.

What about you? Are you living in victory in your current season? Or are you finding it hard to get past some things of last season or even having trouble because you are concerned about tomorrow's season?

With every move we have made, it takes me a while to embrace being "all in" where I am. I always have a few months of working out what happened behind me and what the future will hold, instead of enjoying the present season. However, my husband surprises me every time. He quickly embraces the season we are in and I notice obvious successes as he does. I've heard more than once, Jim Elliot's quote, "Wherever you are, be all there! Live to the hilt every situation you believe to be the will of God."

As in any great story, we find things don't always stay the same. Right at the time when everything seems to be going better for Joseph, another layer of the story unfolds. Read Genesis 39:6-10.

What did Potiphar's wife want?

How did Joseph respond?

Let's first take a look at Potiphar's wife and how her temptation led to sin and brought forth much hurt. Most of us, if watching this un-fold on the big screen, would see ourselves as Joseph, the one who chose what was right. But, go with me here for a minute so we can gain some truth from what we see. Imagine being Potiphar's wife at home and alone. A young man who is well-built, handsome, and successful in all he does comes into your household (see Genesis 39:6). Potiphar was the captain of the guard, so I would assume he is very busy and not at home much. "After a while" she took notice of Joseph (see Genesis 39:7). Once she took notice, there was no restraint in how her temptation went straight to sin.

The phrase, "after a while" really stood out to me when reading this text. In our lives, temptation will come at just the opportune time, so we must learn from this text that just because we don't see a friendship, relationship, job, or thing as a temptation, we must continually pray and use the word of God to guard our hearts and minds before it happens. As we talked about in week 3, predetermine what you are going to do.

What did Jesus include in His prayer when teaching the disciples how to pray in Matthew 6:13?

The second phrase that stood out to me was she took notice. Other versions say, "she cast eyes at Joseph." Because we live on planet earth, we too will have times in our lives where our eyes "take notice" of someone or something. When it happens, what does 2 Corinthians 10:5 say to do?

As Martin Luther King Jr. said, "You cannot keep birds from flying over your head, but you can keep them from building a nest in your hair." Who did Joseph say his sin would be against? (Genesis 39:9)

Joseph called it like it was, a great wickedness and a sin against God. We too need to call sin what it is.

What did Potiphar's wife do? (v. 12)

Even though she spoke to him day by day, he decided not to have any part of it. He not only didn't lie with her or heed her, he also chose to run from her. How hard is it for you when temptation is day by day?

Think of the last time you were tempted. Did you find yourself running away from the source or being drawn to it?

What does James 4:7 say?

Let's look more closely at James 1:12-17

What does verse 12 tell us about someone who endures temptation or perseveres under trial?

First, we know there is a progression of our temptation that begins with our desires. Let's look at the progression that James shows us. Verse 13 reminds us that God is not the source of our temptation.

Verse 14 says we are tempted by what?

The Bible goes on to say, "But each one is tempted when he is drawn away by his own desires and enticed. Then, when desire has conceived, it gives birth to sin; and sin, when it is full-grown, brings forth death" (James 1:14-15, NKJV).

Summarize James 1:16

Each of us has desires that God has given us and, "Every good and every perfect gift is from above, coming down from the Father of the heavenly lights, who does not change like shifting shadows" (James 1:17). But before the gift to fulfill our desire in God's way and God's time, the enemy tempts us in these desires to sin. For example, Potiphar's wife had a desire for sex and companionship with a man. Her good and perfect gift was her husband. However, she allowed herself to be dragged away by her evil desire when she took notice of another man. Before we judge her in her sin, let's be carefully reminded, "all have sinned and fallen short of the glory of God" (Romans 3:23). It should cause us such a holy fear when thinking that our temptation, however small it seems, can lead to death.

We learn from Joseph how he was predetermined about the temptation he was facing, calling it a wickedness and sin against God. We too need to be predetermined of what we will do when tempted.

I want to take a moment and remind you that Joseph was a young man who was alone and had desires of his own. God had just rescued Him from death and the pit, and had placed him in a good position. When he had no one, God was there. What do you think kept Joseph from giving in?

Read Genesis 39:11-18. But one day "it" happened. What happened? How did Joseph respond when the temptation caught him?

There are days when we need to flee. The enemy is very sly. He knows your weakest area. He knows temptation. He began tempting Eve in the garden and he is not going to stop with you. He's looking for those followers who love the Lord their God. He is out to make you fall because that would hurt God and hurt your witness. Joseph had said, "No," to Potiphar's wife and even stated it would be wickedness and a sin against God, but the enemy did not give up. The enemy set the stage in Joseph's life and he can set the stage in your life. Perhaps the time when no one else is around, an opportune time has come. But you, like Joseph are walking in the spirit and have a spirit of wisdom. You will recognize temptation and what could happen if you don't flee.

What does 1 Corinthians 10:13?

God always, and I mean always, makes a way of escape. Ask for it and take it! The enemy is out to take what God has given us. Run! Our God is a jealous God. Don't be deceived as Eve was. Don't think for a minute that Eve wasn't wholeheartedly devoted to God. She was deceived and you can be to. That is why you have to pray for discernment and heed the wisdom God gives you.

Look back at 1 Corinthians 10:12 and write out in your own words what it says.

Some of the most intense temptations for me occurred when I was experiencing heights with God. The enemy would like to take down many with the fall of one, so continue to pray with a Spirit of humility so you are not deceived.

Read Genesis 39:19-23.

Give a brief summary of these verses

Again, someone else's sin affected Joseph. What Joseph didn't know was God was using every bit of this to humble him and prepare him for His promise land. Even in prison, God showed Joseph favor and mercy. The prison guard gave Joseph the position over all the others. You serve a God who is all powerful. He can take the worst of situations and turn them into His glory. We can be a part of that blessing and glory if we will choose to not give in, even in the most intense situations.

I'm thankful Joseph did not give in to Potiphar's wife. "The fear of the LORD is the beginning of wisdom, and knowledge of the Holy One is understanding" (Proverbs 9:10, NKJV). Let it be said of us that we fear our God and we love Him so much that we are not willing to leave His arms for the arms of someone or something sinful. I want to take a moment to say your temptation is always handcrafted by the enemy for you. The temptation doesn't have to be a person. Ask God if there is any area that you are easily deceived by and ask Him to give you wisdom to recognize and turn from this sin.

Knowing that Jesus Himself was tempted in every way yet without sin is important because we tend to think being tempted is sin and something to be ashamed of. This is important to note because **temptation is not sin**. **The sin comes when we yield to the temptation**. Choose loyalty to your God, just as Joseph did.

Looking at our key scripture

"For we do not have a high priest who is _____ to sympathize with _____

weaknesses, but we have one who has been _____ in every way, just as we

are – yet was_____ sin" (Hebrews 4:15).

In His Time

"But those who wait on the LORD, Shall renew their strength; they shall mount up with wings like eagles, They shall run and not be weary; They shall walk and not faint." ~ Isaiah 40:31 NKJV

I like to use Splenda in my coffee. However, yesterday I was all out and I thought, "I'm all out, now I need a substitute for my Splenda." The irony of it all is when I'm out, I use sugar for a substitute. Sugar is the real deal and Splenda is a "substitute" for sugar, not vice versa. It got me to thinking. When is the last time you have said, "I'm all out of _____ in my life and only then you turn to Jesus and draw near to Him. He became the substitute, but just like me you realize as you draw near to Him, He is the real thing and what you are all out of was always the substitute. I say all of this because in every season of our lives we need a real living Savior on a new day. Before we dive into Joseph's life today, read Psalm 20:7. What does it say?

Some trust in chariots and some in horses, but we trust in the name of the LORD our God.

Psalm 20:7

As you go through today's lesson, ask the Lord if there is any area where you are trusting in a substitute.

We left off yesterday with Joseph in prison, and "The keeper of the prison did not look into anything that was under Joseph's authority, because the LORD was with him; and whatever he did, the LORD made it prosper" (Genesis 39:23, NKJV).

Let's start by reading Genesis 40:1-23

We have two new people entering Joseph's life. Who are they and what led them to join Joseph in prison?

_____   _____

Look at verse 40:1 below and stare at the underlined words with me,

"It came to pass after these things that the butler and the baker of the king of Egypt offended their lord, the king of Egypt" (Genesis 40:1, NKJV). I just want to stop here and remind you to keep praying, keep believing. You never know when the time will come when you can look back and say, "it came to pass after these things."

What happened to the butler and baker in verse 5?

What did the butler and baker tell Joseph in verse 8?

How did Joseph respond? (v. 8)

Write out the chief butler's dream and Joseph's interpretation below (verses 9-13).

Dream	Interpretation

What did Joseph ask the butler for in verse 14?

What did Joseph tell the butler in verse 15?

Write out the chief baker's dream and Joseph's interpretation below (verses 16-19).

Dream	Interpretation

We could all agree that prison would seem to be an all-time low point. But instead of being a place of confinement, God used the prison to connect Joseph to two men to the most powerful man in all of Egypt.

What happened in verses 20-22?

If I was Joseph, I would have been on pins and needles waiting for the butler to tell Pharaoh about me. However, verse 23 tells us the time for Joseph had not come. What does verse 23 say?

Often times people will let us down, but God Has Not Forgotten You or me! God did not forget Joseph, even though man did. God was still in control in Joseph's life and He is still in control of our lives. I don't know much about art, but I do love one kind of art called pointillism. The reason I love pointillism so much is because it is a beautiful picture made completely out of small, distinct dots of color applied in patterns to form an image. God is the artist in our lives and He has a vision for each of us. We cannot see how all the dots will connect to make a beautiful work in our lives, but He does. Like Joseph, we must continue to trust and obey when we have to wait for God's timing.

Although we have the advantage of knowing what God was doing in Joseph's life, Joseph did not know that in two years God would change his life and do something exceedingly abundantly more than he could have dreamed. Even without this foresight, he remained faithful.

Let's continue by moving forward to Genesis 41. Start by reading verse 1.

Verse 41:1 starts off with similar wording as chapter 40:1, "it came to pass." Both times, something was about to happen. When was the last time in your life you said, "Then it came to pass?" You've prayed and waited and then one day life is not routine, something changes. Something happens, a memory is triggered and a life is changed.

How many years had Joseph waited before Pharaoh had his dream? (v. 1)

Chapter 41:1 says, "After the end of two full years Pharaoh had a dream. Who was the author of the butler and baker's dreams? _____ Who authored Pharaoh's dream? _____

Read Chapter 41:2-38. How many dreams did Pharaoh have? (v. 5)

Who did Pharaoh send for? What happened when they came? (v. 8)

What did the butler tell Pharaoh in verses 9-14?

Finally, the moment we have been waiting for. The butler may have forgotten Joseph, but God didn't. God could have allowed Pharaoh to have the dream sooner than 2 years after the butler was released, but instead this was God's timing. I don't understand why, but God has a bigger plan and purpose in the length and timing of our trials. When God says it's time, He moves quickly. God was about to promote Joseph to lead the nation of Egypt and in turn would affect the nation of Israel, God's chosen people. He wanted Joseph completely humble and ready for such a position as this.

Look at verse 15. What did Pharaoh say to Joseph that could have caused Joseph to take the opportunity to promote himself?

How did Joseph respond? (v.16)

List the gifts, abilities, strengths, talents, and wisdom you have been given. This could even include positions, family, and your wealth.

Now look back at the list. If someone was reading your story, would they say you have all of these things and lift your name up or would they say, God has given you all this and you use them for His glory?

Now, look at verse 33-38. Did Joseph ever suggest that he should be the one put in charge because it's obvious he is the wise and discerning man Pharaoh needs?

This is challenging and convicting because after such a long wait and finally being brought up out of the pit, it would be tempting to say, "I'm the one you need. Look no further, because God has given me all this and you need me." Instead, Joseph took a place of humility and did not assume such a position. Why did he not have to? And why do you not have to?

Humble yourselves, therefore, under God's mighty hand, that he may lift you up in due time.
1 Peter 5:6

What does 1 Peter 5:6 say?

Glance at Genesis 41:25, 28, and 32, who did Joseph continually point Pharaoh to?

A great leader of God will give credit where credit is due. Just like Daniel, Joseph knew and was unashamed to tell Pharaoh that it was not him, but God who had the answers. Wow! The dream and the interpretation were very detailed and clear. It took a lot of faith for Joseph to interpret the dream and be so bold in what was to come.

Continue to read the rest of Genesis 41:39-57. What happened in verses 39-45?

Joseph never suggested that he would take control over the matters for Pharaoh. What does Philippians 2:3 say?

God is the One who not only pulled Joseph out of slavery and prison, but placed him as 2nd highest in Egypt, under Pharaoh. You, too, serve that God. Our God is the King of kings, and Lord of lords. He is able to pull you out of the pit, out of bondage, and out of your prison. And not just pull you out, but place you wherever He wants.

Most of the time when we read this story, we focus on the fact that Joseph finally made it. The best part of his life was being second – in - command in command to Pharaoh and all the blessings that he received. But I believe our God looks at Joseph's life a little differently. I believe He didn't think the greatest part of Joseph's life was when he was 2nd in command, but all the faithfulness that Joseph had throughout His journey to get there; when he chose not to be bitter toward his brothers and Potiphar's wife, when he chose to work hard when he had every human right to give up or whine and complain, when he chose not to question God's goodness, but quickly gave God the credit for the gift that He was given. He served God and he served people. How old was Joseph when he stood before Pharaoh, king of Egypt? (verse 46)

Wow, did you figure up the time he was given a promise by God and when the promise was fulfilled. He began his journey at 17 and stood before Pharaoh at age 30. I cannot help but think of David, in the book of Samuel, who was anointed to be king at a young age, but wasn't given kingship until about 14 years later. Think about Jesus, who is our God Almighty. He was seen in the temple asking questions and speaking with the priests at age 12, (see Luke 2:46), but didn't begin His ministry until age 30 (see Luke 3:23). Why in the world do we think that we should be any different! I know we get excited and cannot wait to conquer the world, but before David killed the giant, he had to first kill the bear and lion. God is framing up some things for you to do and to have, but remember He is also framing you up to be ready and willing to receive these things. He loves you too much and has too much at stake in your life and the lives of others to give you something before you're ready. If you received it too soon, you wouldn't have the spiritual ability to keep it. He also wants to prepare you, so you don't become prideful and think you are the reason for your success.

The world gets so caught up in trying to become friends or gain relationships to promote self, but the only One you need to know to get where you are meant to go is Jesus. We can get caught up in all the details of how and when of what we want. However, God wants us to serve Him wholeheartedly in today's season. Let God be God over those things. Be found faithful in Him today just as Joseph was.

Take a minute to reflect on your current season of life. Maybe like Joseph, you feel you've been betrayed, sold out, cast in a pit, or thrown into a prison. Maybe everything is well with you this season, but you have become complacent in serving God. Here is your opportunity to renew your trust and ask God to help you be faithful in what He has called you to do today. Maybe you need to stop spending so much time on how He is going to bring about what He has promised and focus on being faithful in what you have promised Him in the season you find yourself currently in.

And while you are being faithful, remember our scripture today.

"But those who _____ on the _____, Shall renew their _____; they

_____ mount up with wings like eagles, They_____ run and not be weary;

They _____ walk and not faint." (Isaiah 40:31, NKJV).

Face to Face

"You intended to harm me, but God intended it for good to accomplish what is now being done, the saving of many lives."
~ Genesis 50:20

I will be the first one to tell you that I know living out your obedience and faith in God is not always easy. Today is one of those days. Joseph knows hard. He has proven himself to be a man of faith, integrity, and godliness. But, he is about to come face to face with an unsettled matter in his life and he has a choice to make. You too are going to be challenged as you move forward in your journey with obedience to God. There will be times that you have to wrestle out the thing with God and surrender to Him, even when it comes to your greatest hurts.

Open to Genesis 42 and read verses 1-24.

And you thought your family had drama. I always want us to be ever so mindful that the people we are reading about are real people of God who are much like us. They have feelings and insecurities. They really have had to make the choices to believe God and do hard things as a follower of Christ. You don't get to where Joseph and other spiritual giants are by easy roads. Maybe that is freedom for someone right now. I will be the first to say, I thought becoming a Christian meant everything in my life would be great from that point on, but oh how naïve I was. However, looking back, I would never be where I am with God and believe and love Him the way I do, if I hadn't experienced trials and tribulations. There is no room for worry in moving forward with God. He knows the measure of grace we need during the hardest points in our lives.

I encourage you to take the time to read all of Genesis 42 through 50. But for today's lesson, we are going to focus on certain points that highlight Joseph's faith and forgiveness. The prophecy of Pharaoh's dream has come true. There were seven years of abundance, when Joseph gathered as much as he was able and managed it well in preparation for the seven years of famine. Amazing how if we will choose to listen to God and be led by His spirit, we will be prepared in and out of season. Genesis 42 begins with Joseph's family feeling the effects of the famine.

What does Genesis 42:1-2 say?

Do you wonder why they looked at each other? Don't you think it was because they thought about Joseph and where he was taken? Now, they had to go to the very place they wanted to avoid.

Is there a place or a situation in your life that makes you nervous just thinking about? Why

I am so thankful we serve a God who is Sovereign and purposeful. Do you ever think that Joseph woke up that morning and thought, "today I will come face to face with my brothers?"

How did Joseph respond to this encounter in Genesis 42:24?

_____

Do not judge, and you will not be judged. Do not condemn, and you will not be condemned. Forgive, and you will be forgiven. Luke 6:37

I'm trying to imagine what that face to face encounter must have been like. Can you think of a time you have forgiven someone in your heart, but then the day comes when you come face to face with that person? I can think of specific times in my life that God didn't just want to leave the forgiveness in my heart. He knew for me to truly heal - I was going to have to face them.

Luke 6:37 tells us in order to receive forgiveness, we must forgive others. There are times in our lives when giving forgiveness is not possible in our own strength. We must surrender our hurt to God and choose forgiveness in obedience to Him.

My little boy Elijah loves Sunday school. However, one time when he was three, he went to a different class and when I came to pick him up, he walked out with his hand in the air and said, "Not good, not good." I was so embarrassed. There are times when it is too much for us to handle. We want to walk out with God and say, "Too hard, it's just too hard." But God often brings us to a point where we are unable to go on without Him.

He does not treat us as our sins deserve or repay us according to our iniquities.

Psalm 103:10

We receive strength to go on as we consider the mercy we have received through God's forgiveness toward us.

Write what Psalm 103:10 says.

What does Luke 23:34 say?

Look back at Luke 23:13-34 and write out what was going on when Jesus said this and who was he talking about?

I remember God revealing this scripture fresh to me the first time when he was calling me to action in forgiving someone who hurt me deeply. There are some hurts you can quickly dismiss, but others penetrate your life so much that it takes years of healing to get through. I'm talking about this kind of hurt. God says, "Forgive them for they know not what they do." You may quickly respond as I did, "Of course, they knew what they were doing to me!" But, spiritually speaking, they hadn't a clue. What may be the most convicting part of this scripture is Jesus forgave you and me for our sin. When he was enduring the torture, physically, mentally, spiritually and emotionally on the cross, we have to remember it was our sin that kept Him there. Once we realize how much our sin cost Him, then our forgiveness of others, no matter how hard, seems possible through His grace and mercy.

Forgiveness has so many effects. I believe it breaks chains between you and that person. It opens up heaven to bless you unlike you've ever seen before and it brings about the redemption of God's people. When we pass off forgiveness as if it doesn't matter, then we have sinned. God does see your hurt and He knows how to heal you. He also has never asked you to do something that He hasn't already done. It's time to let go of that person, so they no longer can have such a hold over you and be that monster in your mind. Trust God and forgive. You will be the one who is free.

I want us to fast forward to Genesis 45 now as we continue with our story of Joseph.

What does verses 5-8 say?

Not only did Joseph choose to forgive, but He chose to see how God was good and sovereign throughout his life. Fast forward to Genesis 50:15-21 and read about Joseph forgiving his brothers. Why were the brothers afraid? (v.15)

What does verse 17 say?

God did not want evil to happen to Joseph, but in His sovereignty and for His greater purpose, He allows it for many to be saved. Think about your own life. Some of the hardest things that have happened in your life, God could use for His greatest glory and purpose in your life to bring many to salvation. God commands us to forgive, but He is not dismissing the fact of what was done to you. Joseph knew something that only God could have instilled in His heart. Read Genesis 50:19-21 and write in your own words what Joseph told his brothers?

Joseph experienced so much between his teenage dreams and his reign in Pharaoh's kingdom. Go with me here as we imagine what Joseph might have thought at this point in his life. All those years before any hurt, trial, or betrayal, he might have been somewhat prideful about the future he imagined in his father's house. But now, I'm sure he's so different. After all these years experiencing God's faithfulness, he recognizes the fulfillment of the dream was so much more than he could have imagined. No longer does he dream of glory and honor for himself among his family. His life has been surrendered to honor and glorify God, serving all of those who so desperately needed His saving power and grace.

What about you? If you are in Christ, you too have a story with eternal significance. Joseph was only able to fulfill God's plan for his life as He completely surrendered to God.

Maybe some of the hardest people to forgive are the ones who are brothers and sisters in Christ, who sinned against you. Many times we say, "Lost people are to act lost, but this was my brother, my sister in Christ." Again, if you find yourself with a deep hurt from someone who you once shared a deep and intimate friendship in Christ, you are in good company with those who have gone before you. Look at what David said about this. "Even my close friend, someone I trusted, one who shared my bread, turned against me" (Psalm 41:9).

Look back at Jesus' time of deepest need. He took Peter, James, and John with Him in the garden as he prayed before going to the cross. He asked them to watch and pray as He did.

What does Matthew 26:40-41 say?

They were physically tired and spiritually asleep on what was ahead. In the box below, write out what we find out about Peter before and after Jesus was arrested.

BEFORE Matthew 26:33-35	AFTER Matthew 26:69-75

Peter loved Jesus deeply and never thought he would deny Jesus. I am so thankful that we can read in John 21:15-19 that Jesus not only forgave Peter completely, but continued to love him and use him in a mighty way for His kingdom. If you walk with God long enough you will find yourself in the place of one who has to forgive unbelievers, enemies, and even dear friends of the faith. But, you also along with the rest of us have been forgiven of much more. Read Matthew 18:21-35. What happened in this story?

Jesus paints the picture of a wicked servant who was forgiven of a large debt, but would not forgive something much smaller. Forgiveness is a serious matter to God and it is not based on feelings, but on the truth of God's Word and we are commanded to forgive, no matter the offense or our feelings.

91

Look back at Matthew 18:21, 22, and 35. What does it say about forgiveness?

End today by asking God if there is anyone you need to forgive or ask forgiveness from? Don't wait any longer in doing what God wants you to do. Start with confessing your heart and thoughts to God. Even if you don't "feel" forgiveness, say out loud, "Jesus, I thank you for forgiving me of all of my sin. I forgive _____, even if I don't feel it. Enable me to obey you as I work out forgiving them in my heart. And if you ask me to take it a step further, please help me to quickly obey You.

As you fill in the blanks below from today's scripture, say it aloud.

"You _____ to harm me, but God _____ it for _____ to

accomplish what is now being done, the _____ of many _____.

Genesis 50:20

Week 5

FINISH WELL

What about when it gets hard

"Therefore He is also able to save to the uttermost those who come to God through Him, since He always lives to make intercession for them." Hebrews 7:25 NKJV

Following Jesus is not always easy. Many times you may feel as if you are dying inside before you experience that abundant life. And really, we are. We are dying to ourselves, so Christ can live through us. Surrendering is one day at a time, walking in obedience and trusting God, even when we don't understand. As you walk in a complete surrender to God, there will be times when events in life happen that are completely beyond your understanding. Remember, in these times, God is completely in control, He loves you, and you can trust Him.

I remember one particular time that I was following Jesus as close as I ever had. And then, "one day it happened." One of those life altering events happened and I found myself in a pit. It is one thing to be in a pit when you messed up and your own sin caused you to be there (and I've done that too), but what about when it is because of your service to the Lord you've been thrown in, cast out, belittled, or betrayed. We are going to spend this week looking into lives that were hit hard by the enemy because of their love for God and their obedience to Him. However, we are also going to see how God proved Himself faithful to them.

Let's begin with the life of Job. Allow yourself to take a ride back in time and engage your mind, spirit and emotions in today's lesson. Pray and ask God to reveal Himself to you. Open to Job chapter one. Let's walk through this together. Read Job 1:1-5

What does verse 1 say about who Job was?

Job had _____ sons and _____ daughters. (v. 2)

Verse 3 says, Job possessed

_____ sheep _____ camels _____ oxen

_____ female donkeys _____ household

Job was called _____ of the East.

What does verses 4 and 5 say about Job?

I'm trying to imagine such a person as Job. He had great influence, wealth, and responsibility, but was still careful to rise early and sacrifice to the Lord on behalf of his children. Job's life reveals to us we can have great responsibility and still uphold the things of God. Many times we make excuses that we are unable to spend time with God - reading our Bible, spending time in prayer, going to church, sharing the gospel with others, and obeying Him - because of our busy lives. However, Job shows us the more we have, the more careful we must be in our faithful discipline in the things of God.

Through the Word we are going to clearly see what was happening in Job's life, both on earth and in heaven. However, Job did not see what we are about to witness.

Continue reading, Job 1:6-12.

Who do we find in the presence of the Lord on this day according to verse 6?

I expected to hear about the angels, but Satan coming before God? What was Satan's purpose in coming to the presence of the Lord at this time? (vs. 7-12)

Read verse 8 and list what God said in His testimony about Job.

God Himself was proclaiming from His throne with everyone in heaven listening, His personal testimony of Job. He didn't just say he was blameless, upright, feared God, and shunned evil, but who did God say was like Job on earth? (v. 8)

God is talking about you in heaven. He has a testimony of you and He says, "Look there is my servant _____(your name). What does this mean to you?

Of course, Satan had his sight on Job. He was the most faithful man of his time. Satan was looking for a way to cause Job to sin. What did Satan answer in verses 9-11?

Here was Job, a man who was like no other on earth and Satan still found a way to accuse him before God. "Does Job fear God for nothing" (Job 1:9). What specific thing did Satan say Job would do in verse 11 if God touched all Job had?

95

God is all powerful and doesn't have to prove anything to Satan. We may be shocked to know how many times Satan has asked for things in our lives and he got a "no." God is not out to harm us in any way. But, He does allow things to happen in our lives to prove us genuine and to refine us for His kingdom purposes. Also, take note that Satan had to ask God, and God gave him limitations.

Read Luke 22:31-32. What did Jesus tell Simon Peter in Luke 22:31?

Both times Satan asks. He wouldn't ask if he had full reign to do whatever he wanted to. However, what did Jesus tell Peter in verse 32?

Read Revelation 12:10. How is Satan referred to?

Just hearing this may cause some of you to want to retreat or be paralyzed in fear. When my son first learned to swim, he learned with flippers. He was so comfortable that when we were staying at a hotel, he jumped in the deep end of a pool without the flippers and immediately started to sink. I completely froze in fear. However, my friend who is a great swimmer and teaches swimming lessons, didn't think twice, but jumped right in and pulled him up. The difference between us was our mental muscle. She had trained for this very situation and I had never even thought this kind of event through. It's necessary for us to train and exercise our spiritual muscle, so we are ready when the spiritual battle comes. What does 2 Timothy 1:7 tell us?

For God has not given us a spirit of fear, but of power and of love and of a sound mind.

(2 Timothy 1:7, NKJV)

Now look back at what you've written and say it out loud. Commit this scripture to memory so you are ready to speak it to yourself when fear arises.

We have an enemy, Satan, who wants to kill, steal, and destroy us (see John 10:10). But our Savior, Jesus Christ, who is over all of life and creation has authority over Satan and He intercedes for us. Jesus knows your name, he knows your needs, your heart's desires and he can be trusted.

Just as in Simon Peter's case, God gives us a heads up that we will all experience trials, tests, and persecution. We have to get our heads out of the sand and not just pass off warfare as if the events happening are just life, but know we have a real enemy. Jesus not only is interceding for us, but has given us weapons of warfare, so we too can be victorious.

Read Romans 8:26-28? Who is making intercession for you?

The Spirit is interceding for you according to what? (v. 27)

Take a moment to look inside your own life. Are you one who would be found always looking for the next accusation against someone or are you found interceding by praying for God's people and the lost according to God's will? Take the time to write who you should be interceding for today.

Revelation 4 and 5 takes us to the throne room of heaven. What does Revelation 5:8 say is in the golden bowls?

We too are invited in to the throne room of God. I'm concerned with the age of technology. We are substituting our glorious and necessary role of joining with God in what He is doing on the kingdom calendar with our own schedule of events, including checking our next text, reading the next status update, sending our next tweet, or running from one activity to the next.

And... Each one had a harp and they were holding golden bowls full of incense, which are the prayers of the saints.

Revelation 5:8

The product of these distractions will not last. But your intercession through prayer lasts for eternity. I guess what is sobering for me is I spend a lot of time talking about changes that I and others need to make. But I'm sad to think how that wasted energy could be profoundly used for the glory of God. Instead of talking, we could be praying with scriptures in hand for each according to God's will. What if prayer was no longer just the prelude to the thing we want to get to; our meal, our day, our activity, and instead became THE MAIN THING.

Who needs you praying for them today: family, friends, lost world, neighborhood, work, church leaders, school, community, state, country, nations? What device do you need to put down, activity you need to do less of, or even sleep do you need to give up to invest that time in prayer?

Read 1 Peter 5:8-9 below and underline the action words that God commands us to do.

"Be self-controlled and alert, your enemy the devil prowls around like a roaring lion looking for someone to devour. Resist him, standing firm in the faith, because you know that your brothers throughout the world are undergoing the same kind of sufferings" (1 Peter 5:8-9).

Like soldiers, we have to realize we are not alone in these experiences, but fellow believers are undergoing the same kind of suffering. Let's look at each of the words you underlined in more detail to get a better understanding of what we are to do. Match the words to the verses.

Be self-controlled   "All men will hate you because of me, but he who stands firm to the end will be saved" (Matthew 10:22).

Alert...   "And pray in the Spirit on all occasions with all kinds of prayers and requests. With this in mind, be alert and always keep on praying for all the saints" (Ephesians 6:18).

Resist him	"Like a city whose walls are broken down is a man who lacks self-control" (Proverbs 25:28).
Standing firm in the faith	"Submit yourselves, then, to God. Resist the devil and he will flee from you" (James 4:7).

Now, turn to Ephesians 6:10-17

Verse 10: Who are we to be strong in and receive our power?

Verses 11, 13: What are we commanded to do and why?

Verse 12: Who are we fighting against?

The enemy is of the spiritual realm. We lose many battles because we make it about a person, when we are not fighting against flesh and blood.

Look at Ephesian 6:14-17 and list the armor of God.

Begin each day putting your armor on. On the way to school each morning, I pray over the kids and myself, "Lord, we put on the helmet of salvation, protect our thinking. We are putting on the breastplate of righteousness, protect our emotions, we are putting on the belt of truth, help us distinguish between what is true and not. We shod our feet with the preparation of the gospel of peace, help us to be ready in season and out. We raise up the sword of the spirit, which is the Word of God, and the shield of faith to quench all the fiery darts of the wicked one. Praying always."

Armed and ready!
Take a look at 1 Peter 5:5-7. What are these scriptures clear about us being?

Humility is necessary for victory. Why?

Read 1 Peter 5:10-11 and circle what it says God will do for you after you have suffered a while.

Make you happy	Give you everything you want	perfect
establish	strengthen	settle

God is after more than us winning our battles, but through our trials he is building in us character and strength so we will look more like Christ and our lives will bring Him much glory. Say this to yourself as you fill in the blanks below.

"Therefore He is also _____ to save to the _____ those who come to God

through Him, since He always _____to make _____ for them"

(Hebrews 7:25, NKJV)

I cannot think of a better way to end today's lesson, than on our knees, laying it all before Him, allowing Him to shower us with mercy and grace in our time of need as He makes intercession for us.

Blessed be the Name of the LORD

"Then Job arose, tore his robe, and shaved his head; and he fell to the ground and worshiped." And he said: 'Naked I came from my mother's womb, And naked shall I return there. The LORD gave, and the LORD has taken away; Blessed be the name of the LORD." ~ Job 1:20 NKJV

As we begin today, let's be reminded of where we left off yesterday. If you haven't already, find a place to humble yourself before God in prayer, casting your cares upon Him and putting on the full armor of God. In your prayer take 2 Timothy 1:7 from yesterday and pray out loud, "God has not given me a spirit of fear, but of power, love and a sound mind" (2 Timothy 1:7, NKJV). We will need to be fully suited up in the armor of God today. We are going to see what took place in heaven in yesterday's lesson, become a reality in today's lesson.

Before we go to our next set of scriptures in Job, I want us to be reminded of what Satan was after from yesterday's lesson. Look Back at Job 1:11-12 and write out what Satan said Job would do when God stretches out his hand and touches all he has?

Now, take a look back at Job 1:5. What specifically does Job say at the end of verse 5 for his reasoning on offering burnt offerings and sacrifices to God on behalf of his children?

Job was careful to go before God on behalf of his sons and daughters, if possibly they have "sinned and cursed God in their hearts" (see Job 1:5). We see Satan go after the very heart of this statement. Not only did Satan say Job would curse God, not just in his heart, but to God's face. I hope you see the fullness of this as I am for the first time. Satan was very specific in what he was after, turning Job's deep devotion of not cursing God even in his children's hearts, to making it come out of His own mouth to God. He wanted to try and prove Job's devotion was conditional, not because it's genuine. Just take away the hedge and he will no longer be devoted to You.

Satan is after the devoted things. Anytime we have something in our life we have devoted to God, we must have the Lord's help. We have to become especially careful in these areas because the testing will become fierce. During our times of testing, it's important we draw near to God and stand on the promises of His Word.

Do you have something specific you have devoted to God and have been careful to give to Him? Have you been tested on this thing? Maybe the hedge around it moved?

Read 2 Timothy 1:12 below and **underline** who will keep what you have committed to God.

"For this reason I also suffer these things; nevertheless I am not ashamed, for I know whom I have believed and am persuaded that He is able to keep what I have committed to Him until that day" (2 Timothy 1:12, NKJV).

Continually commit your devoted things to God and pray His Word, believing what He has promised you. Let's see this unfold in Job's life. Please ask God to give you understanding as you read Job 1:13-22.

"Now there was a day" (see Job 1:13). In all of our lives we can think back to times in our lives that we too would say, "There was a day." We have good days and we can remember back recalling every detail. And then we have those days that come that are not good. I wonder if you are thinking back to one of those very days now. We don't want to be reminded of those days. However, if you have allowed God's healing hand to heal you and bring you even closer to Him because of this trial, you can see how God used what you thought was the worst day of your life to bring about something good.

Read Job 1:13-22 and fill in the blanks of Job's loss.

Messenger	What happened	What was lost
1. (verses 13-15)		
2. (verse 16)		
3. (verse 17)		
4. (verses 18-19)		

Imagine such horrific tragedy in one day. Job didn't just have to endure the tragedy, but Satan set it up in such a way that each time it says, "while he was still speaking, another came." Each one said, "And I alone have escaped to tell you." Satan allows one servant to survive to tell Job the news. This happens consecutively four times. The enemy knows how to kick us when we are down. He purposely left one to tell Job the bad news in succession.

What does Job 1:20-21 say?

Satan lost what he was after in these two verses. Job did not sin or curse God, but worshiped God and blessed His name. Now that is a man who loves and trusts his God. Satan had lost, but he was not done. Job chapter 2 brings another day in heaven. The scene looks much like the last one. Read Job 2:1-3

What question did God ask Satan both times he presented himself before the Lord?

No temptation has overtaken you except such as is common to man; but God is faithful, who will not allow you to be tempted beyond what you are able, but with the temptation will also make the way of escape, that you may be able to bear it.
1 Corinthians 10:13

We know God knows everything, so why do you think He ask him this question?

God knew exactly where Satan had been. This reveals to us the relationship between God and Satan. Sometimes we put Satan in the ring with God as an equal match. But these verses indicate there is no equal match. Satan presents himself before the Lord. He has to answer God when asked a question. And he has been given limitations.

What does God say to Satan in verse 3 about Job?

God gave His testimony of Job and added something new. "...and still he holds fast to his integrity, although you incited Me against him, to destroy him without a cause" (Job 2:3, NKJV). God did not pass over what had happened to Job, but He had a close eye on Job. Notice the phrase, "without a cause." God not only takes notice, but feels it to. This is all the more reason for us to be faithful. God knew Job's heart and He knows your heart.

Remember 1 Corinthians 10:13 from last week's homework. Take a look at it in the margin and write what stands out fresh to you today.

Job is about to enter another battle that he knows nothing about. Satan cannot touch God, so instead Satan comes after what's most precious to God, the people who love God.

Now read Job 2:4-10

What did Satan ask God to do in verse 5?

What specifically did Satan want Job to do? (v. 5)

At the end of verse 5, he says, "...and he will surely curse You to Your face" (Job 2:5, NKJV)! Again, he was after the same thing, but this time he wanted to add physical turmoil to what Job was already experiencing mentally and emotionally.

However, verse 6 shows us God's sovereignty over the situation. What did God tell Satan at the end of verse 6?

Interestingly, Satan spared Job's wife in the first attack when he was given permission to take all that Job had. The only instruction given to Satan was he could not take Job's life. Why do you think he spared Job's wife?

Job's wife would have been the closest person to him of all people. She too would have lost all her children, wealth, and servants. Job was hurting from his own loss, but to watch his wife grieving as well, would be pain upon pain. She also would be a voice to Job and someone Satan could use to try and persuade him. What did Job's wife say in verse 9?

Not only did Satan want her to tempt Job to curse God to his face, but to lose the very thing God told Satan Job was holding fast to (his integrity).

It is easy to "go emotional" on someone during times of testing. When everything around us seems like it is falling apart, we must allow God to tend to our hearts and quiet our souls. I am not going to be the first to throw stones at Job's wife. Until you have walked in someone's shoes, you cannot know what it is like. I wish I could sit here and tell you that I've always got it right, but that's not the case.

What was Job's response to his wife? (verse 10)

So then, my beloved brethren, let every man be swift to hear, slow to speak, slow to wrath; James 1:19, NKJV

Job was in deep pain. His anguish was mental, physical, emotional, on every level. He did not understand the reasons for such tragedy in his life, but he did not blame God in anyway. God had not changed, even though Job's circumstances had. And Job realized this.

Let's look together at a few scriptures that will help us.

What does James 1:19 say?

When we are up against a fierce battle, we have to speak truth to our souls and tame our tongues. James tells us we have the power of life and death in our tongues. We can see how Job and his wife's responses were different in the same circumstances.

How do you see yourself responding when the fight is hard? Do you want to blame God or others, or do you want to ask the Lord to help you through it?

Read Psalm 62, a psalm of David. What did he say in verses 1-2 and 5-7?

What did David instruct us to do in verse 8?

Look at our key scripture and fill in the blanks

"Then Job arose, tore his robe, and shaved his head; and he _____ _____ _____

_____ and _____." And he said: 'Naked I came from my mother's

womb, And naked shall I return there. The LORD gave, and the LORD has taken away;

_____ be the _____ of the _____" (Job 1:20 NKJV)

The two responses that stare back at me the most are;

Fell to the ground and worshiped   Blessed be the Name of the LORD

I'm sure Job had to make the conscience choice to worship and praise God's name in a time like this. Often times our first reactions will set the tone for what follows in our attitudes during our trials. My son asked me today, when talking about a matter of obedience, "What if I don't feel it?" I responded, "We cannot always respond based on feelings, but we have to choose to obey despite how we feel."

I believe and therefore I speak

"I know that my Redeemer lives, and that in the end he will stand upon the earth." ~ Job 19:25

As I pray about today's lesson, I try to imagine your current circumstances. Can you remember a time you experienced a low point in your life and you didn't have a friend to walk alongside you? Perhaps you find yourself in that place today.

We've all had those people in our lives who we would consider acquaintances; but, what about that friend who is willing to travel the distance to comfort you in your time of greatest need? Do you have a friend like that?

What does Proverbs 18:24 say?

What about you? Are you that kind of friend to someone?

As we continue to walk through Job's life today, we are going to find that sometimes God has given us friends who are willing to go the distance with us, but these friends cannot fully comprehend the depth of your needs, mentally, physically, and spiritually. God reserves the right to bring you to Himself during these trials, so when you see the victory you are drawn to Him more and more and not man. I hope this encourages you. Don't think that your friends have abandoned you. Instead know God is too wise to give you what you think you may need, so He can be all you need. I remember one instance where God brought me to a lonely place during a time of deepest need. I looked around and thought, "Where is everybody?" In that season, I could have been given over to bitterness, but God was faithful. At that time, I had a CD by Jeremy Camp and would hear the song, "Just Give Me Jesus." I pray in today's lesson, you too can say, "Just give me Jesus."

A man who has friends must himself be friendly, But there is a friend who sticks closer than a brother. (Proverbs 18:24, NKJV)

Open up to Job chapter 2 and let's start there. Read Job 2:11-13.

List the names of Job's friends and where they are from?

Verse 11 tells us about three friends. Each had heard about all of Job's troubles and set out to meet up and go to Job. What two things did they plan to do when they got to Job? (v. 11)

It is one thing to hear about something, but to experience it is altogether different. When the United States experienced the tragic events of 9/11, I only saw and heard about what had happened on TV. Later, I listened to the book on tape, "Let's Roll," by Lisa Beamer. Her husband, Todd Beamer, was one of the courageous passengers on United Airlines flight 93 that went down on 9/11. I couldn't get through a chapter without crying. But something happened when I was in New York and went to ground zero and visited the new opening of the 9/11 museum. I know I cannot put it in words, but when I walked up to the very place of memorial and saw it with my own eyes, I was taken back. When I walked in the museum, I was so overwhelmed with emotion I began to cry before I saw one thing. Even so, nothing could compare with those who lived in New York and lived out these events personally.

Job's friends had heard of what happened to Job, but nothing prepared them for what they would see. Read Job 2:12 and write in your own words what happened when the friends saw Job from a distance.

"They sat on the ground with Job for _____ days and

_____ nights without _____, because they

saw how great his suffering was" (Job 2:13).

Recently, our pastor preached a message about the stages of grief. One thing I remember him saying is it is good to show up and not say anything. "Show up and shut up." We laughed when he said it in this way, but that is a good way to remember what to do when you are going to comfort someone. The best way is to say nothing, just be there for them. If verse 13 ended with what we heard about Job's friends then time well spent; but, unfortunately, as soon as Job opens his mouth to speak, his friends took it upon themselves to tell Job what they thought about his suffering. Each of these three friends, Eliphaz, Bildad, and Zophar took it upon themselves to tell Job he was suffering because of sin and needed to repent. You can find their conversations in Job 3 through 31. After these three speak, another man, who was standing by began to speak. His response is given in Job 32-37. He believed God was using Job's suffering to mold and train Job and this young man thought he had wisdom that the others didn't have.

Read Job 16:2-5 and summarize what Job said to his friends

After reading their conversations, I think, "What if?" What if Job's friends spent all those words not rebuking Job, but praying over Job. I just imagine how different things would have been if one by one, each friend called on the Name of the LORD and petitioned God on behalf of Job.

Read Job 19:13-22. Who stood with Job during this time of greatest trial and loss.

What did Paul say in 2 Timothy 4:16-18?

The apostle Paul said, "I want to know Christ and the power of his resurrection and the fellowship of sharing in his sufferings, becoming like him in death, and so, somehow, to attain to the resurrection from the dead" (Philippians 3:10).

How do you think what Paul and Job were experiencing allowed them to fellowship in the sufferings of Christ?

There is much fruit that comes from our seasons of sufferings. Read 2 Timothy 4:7-8 and list the what three things Paul said he had done.

I have...

What did he say was in store for him and for all those who long for Christ appearance?

When I think of Job's conversations with his friends, I think about a time when my life seemed to be falling apart. I remember seeking counsel from someone who should have been encouraging me to "fight the good fight, finish the race, keep the faith,"; but instead, he gave no hope. Even though I was very young in my faith and had never experienced this kind of warfare, God had given me scriptures that I kept with me. After he voiced no hope over my situation, I pulled out these scriptures and I said, "But my God says" ... and I recited each one of those scriptures. I learned in that dark season, the great power of the spoken Word of God. My God was faithful and He came through in that situation, just as He has been faithful throughout my entire life. This is what we see with Job. By Job's friends questioning his faith, it gave Job an opportunity to stand on faith in God alone.

Let's be careful when we encounter times where people around us are going through difficult situations.

Read Proverbs 10:19 Who does this scripture say is wise?

What does Psalm 19:14 say?

Many times our words are "good to us or to those who agree with us", but are they pleasing to God?

May the words of my mouth and the meditation of my heart be pleasing in your sight, O LORD, my Rock and my Redeemer.

Psalm 19:14NIV

Job and his friends didn't know about the conversation between Satan and God. What if you knew that your present trouble started out as a heavenly conversation and God gave a testimony of you in heaven of your blamelessness, righteousness, and integrity? How would you feel?

Read Hebrews 12:1-2. What does verse 1 say?

There are many people watching you walk out your life with Christ, especially in your most trying times. When you choose to persevere and finish well, many lives will be affected, bringing God much glory.

What does Hebrews 12:2 say?

As you fill in today's key verse, claim it as Job faithfully did.

"I know that my _____ _____, and that in the end _____ will

_____ upon the earth" (Job 19:25).

Who is Like Our God?

"As the heavens are higher than the earth, so are my ways higher than your ways and my thoughts than your thoughts." Isaiah 55:9

Have you ever been in a situation in life and the Word you get from the Lord, is "Be still and know I am God." Psalm 46:10

I have a friend who has a golden retriever. He can put a piece of food on the dog's nose and say, "Wait for it, wait for it... Go." And the dog waits for the exact second of the word "Go", before taking the food.

In your life, are you willing to, "Wait for Him, wait for Him" or do you find yourself on "Go?" Explain.

We need to be a people who are willing to "wait for God's clear instruction" but also be willing to "go" when He says go. I would say most of us in the flesh fall into one of two categories. Some of us are okay with waiting, but not so willing to go, while others of us are ready to go, but have a hard time waiting for God's timing.

Today's lesson reminds me of such a case. In yesterday's lesson there was a lot of talking going on over Job's life. Does it matter what everybody else thinks, if we haven't heard from God Himself? Today is one of those days to sit and listen. God is going to show up on the scene of Job's life. I believe we and Job are going to receive more than we ask for. How is this possible! Because our God is more than we could even dream up or imagine.

I pray today's lesson moves you as it does me. I've always heard that the awe of God proceeds faith. Let's take a look. Open up to Job, chapter 38 begins with God speaking to Job. Read Job 38:1.

The LORD answered Job out of the _____.

God answered Job out of the whirlwind. God was not waiting for the friends to finish, so He could be next in the conversation. God was waiting for the exact time that **He had set to reveal Himself to Job**.

I believe it's important to your faith that you take the time and read what God says to Job. Read Job 38-39. The scriptures today may seem long, but thank God that we are being invited in to see Him on a higher level of understanding as God speaks to Job.

Take time to list five things that you would say stood out to you the most in these two chapters.

1. _____

2. _____

3. _____

4. _____

5. _____

Job 38:22 would be something that stands out to me, "Have you entered the storehouses of the snow or seen the storehouses of the hail." If there has ever been a time that this scripture has popped off the page and into my life it would be in the last 7 months; a whirlwind indeed. Over and over God would lead me to was Job 38. I remember driving and seeing small flakes of snow coming down. Each one would melt as soon as it hit the windshield or ground. As I watched the snowflakes fall and melt, the Lord reminded me, "Just because you don't see the snow, doesn't mean I don't have a storehouse for it." About a month later, we experienced the biggest snow I had ever seen personally. I remember thinking it wasn't going to snow from the looks outside. However, the weather channel said we were supposed to get six inches. Instead we got twelve inches! Again, I was reminded, "just because you don't see the snow, doesn't mean I don't have a storehouse for it." I wonder how you would answer this question.

Just because I haven't seen _____

doesn't mean that God is unable to do it.

What does Proverbs 3:5-6 say?

As long as you and I are on this earth, we will never fully understand who God is and why He allows what He does. He is God and I am so thankful for that. I am glad that He controls the snow, wind, and rain. I'm glad He has control over everything. We serve an eternal God. He is not just the God over the beginning of time to the end, but He is the God outside of time. We think in terms of time, but God is eternal and He thinks in light of eternity. This is too much for our human mind to comprehend. That's why our faith is so important.

Read Job 40:1-5

After God spoke to Job in chapters 38-39, what did Job say and do in Job 40:3-5?

Continue reading the rest of chapter 40 and 41.

What were some things the Lord said and how did that relate to God's sovereignty and strength?

Let's continue with the last chapter in Job. Read Job 42:1-6.

What did Job say in verse 2?

verse 5?

What did Job do as a result? (verse 6)

Even Job, who was called by God blameless and who exhibited his faith to others was able to see himself more clearly in the light of God now. He experienced God's strength, majesty, and great sovereignty in a way he had never before.

But, let him who boasts boast in the Lord.

2 Corinthians 10:17

I am reminded of 2 Corinthians 10 verses 12 and 17. Who does verse 12 say is not wise?

Who should our boasting be in? (v. 17)

Job was about to get a huge turn-around in life. He had been hit hard. However, God will never waste these times in our lives. Even the times that we want to give up, God uses to show us Himself in a greater way than ever before.

And then, just at the right time, He reaches out His hand and lifts up out of the pit.

Read the following verses and fill in the chart.

Scripture	God's Action	Our Action	Eternal results
Psalm 40: 1-3			

Job was about to be lifted up and a new song would be put in his mouth. Before we see God address Job and his future, let us look back at his friends. Remember, Job's friends started off well by sitting for seven days and nights without saying a word, but it went downhill from there. Now, let's take a look at what God said to Job's friends who thought they had all the right answers and were right with God, while they thought Job was tied up in sin the whole time. Read Job 42:7-9.

What did God say to Job's friends? (v. 7)

What did God tell them to do as a result? (v. 8)

God told them to go to Job, but this time not to give opinions. Instead, to confess their wrong and receive God's grace, by Job praying for them. For Job's friends and Job, this act of obedience would have done a work in both. How might these events sanctify Job and his friends? List anything that comes to mind.

Job's friends:

Job:

God designed it for the friend's repentance with God and Job's future prosperity to come about through this very specific event. It would have taken a great deal of humility for Job's friends to go to Job for prayer. But even more so, how hard was it for Job to face those friends and pray for their forgiveness. We all may find ourselves on either side in life. There will be times that you will have to humble yourself and say, "I am so sorry, please forgive me. I was wrong." But other times, we will have to also allow God to tend our hurts and bitterness and pray for those who have hurt us. Job could have been like we are so many times when we are in the pit and those around us take a negative look at us. He could have carried some unforgiveness, but he didn't.

What does Job 42:10 say?

It was after Job's obedience to pray for his friends that God made him prosperous again and gave him twice as much as he had before. We have a lot to gain if we are obedient like Job was. This was not a time for pride or bitterness. Job had already lost too much. This was a time of restoration and rebuilding. We too have a lot to lose by wearing a badge of hurt, un-forgiveness, and growing bitter. And we have a lot to gain by forgiving, praying, and moving forward with God, trusting Him to make all wrongs right in His way and His time.

What if God is saying to you as He did Job, only after you pray, then you will be restored. Would you be willing to stop the blessings of God in your life because of your own hurt and stubbornness? God knows all too well, in order for us to move forward freely with Him, we must make right what He asks of us. Remember back to Job 42:5-6, when Job first saw who he was in light of the Lord's presence.

Is there anyone, when their name is mentioned, you cringe and think, "I not only don't want to pray for them, I think they don't deserve my prayers and forgiveness?"

Consider Job when he realized who he was in comparison to God's greatness. Only when you and I encounter God are we able to pray and forgive others who hurt us deeply. We see more clearly that we too had a debt we could not pay.

But God demonstrates his own love for us in this: While we were still sinners, Christ died for us.

Romans 5:8

What does Romans 5:8 say?

How hard do you think it was for Christ to come and live on earth in a human body, endure every temptation and trial, and surrender His life completely over to death for you and me?

There are always blessings waiting on the other side of obedience. Job was about to see a total restoration. He wasn't going to get the old back, but God was doing a new thing and it would be double what he had before. Take a look in Job 42:10-17. What did God do for Job after he prayed for his friends?

"And the God of all grace, who called you to his eternal glory in Christ, after you have suffered a little while, will himself restore you and make you strong, firm, and steadfast. To him be the power for ever and ever. Amen" (1 Peter 5:10-11).

Look again at today's key verse and fill in the blanks of what God tells us.

"As the _____ are higher than the _____, so are _____ ways

higher than _____ ways and _____ thoughts than _____ thoughts" (Isaiah 55:9).

Take a look back at Week 2, Day 5 at the prayer you wrote out. Record on Week 2, Day 5 in the provided spaces how God has worked in answering your prayer.

Glory to Come

"I consider that our present sufferings are not worth comparing with the glory that will be revealed in us." ~ Romans 8:18

Just as Job provides an Old Testament example of faithfulness to God in trying times, John The Baptist provides an example for us in the New Testament. Let's begin by getting a glimpse into who John is and His purpose on the kingdom calendar. Read Mark 1:1-8 and write what description this scripture tells us about who John is and the purpose of his life and ministry.

Now take a look at Isaiah 40:3 and Malachi 3:1. What do these two scriptures tell us?

Jesus answered, "I am the way the truth and the life. No one comes to the Father, except through me."

John 14:6

God had given the prophecy through these scriptures that He would send a messenger, to prepare the way. Messengers were sent ahead of Kings to remove any obstacles for the king's journey. John the Baptist was sent by God to prepare the way for the Way. Read John 14:6. What does Jesus say about Himself in this verse?

What did the people surrounding John the Baptist's birth say about him in Luke 1:66?

"Now his father Zacharias was filled with the Holy Spirit, and prophesied, saying..." (Luke 1:67, NKJV). Read what He prophesied in Luke 1:68-79 and write out what stands out to you.

"So the child grew and became strong in spirit, and was in the desert till the day of his manifestation to Israel" (Luke 1:80, NKJV).

God's people were waiting and watching for the coming of the Messiah. It had been 400 years since they had heard from God. Read Matthew 3:1-4.

Where did John preach? (verse 1)

What was John's message? (verse 2)

What description does verse 4 give about John?

Continue reading Matthew 3:5-12 and give a brief description of what was taking place.

John was moving forward in the ministry God had called him to do and prepared him for. God has a purpose for each of us also. As we can see from the scripture, John didn't have the average look or diet of a preacher. But one thing was for sure, His message pointed to Only One and His name is Jesus.

What did John say about Jesus in Matthew 3:11

Read Matthew 3:13-15

Why was John trying to deter Jesus from being baptized by him? (v.14)

What was Jesus' response to him in verse 15?

Can you imagine being John at this moment? You are baptizing those who are coming to you, being careful to tell them that you are not the Messiah, but preparing the way for the One to come. You even point out that you are not even worthy to do the most menial task for Him. And then it happens. Jesus comes and says, "I want you to baptize Me," the greatest honor on earth.

Think how he must have felt as he stepped into the water with Jesus. Holding onto him and going through the baptism ceremony that he had done so many times before. Each time significant, but no other could even compare. This time it was His Lord and Savior, Jesus Christ.

Continue reading Matthew 3:16-17

What happened after Jesus was baptized that revealed to John and to us that Jesus is the Son of God?

Can you think of an experience you have had with Jesus that is personal to you? A time when you experienced Him in an intimate way and He showed you how much He thinks of you?

John spent his whole ministry preparing people for Jesus. When Jesus walked on the scene, he was careful to point those who followed him to Jesus. Take a look at John 1:35-42. Who was following the teachings of John and what did John say to them when he saw Jesus? (v. 35)

What happened after that? (vs. 37-42)

How much does your life look like John the Baptist's life? Do you spend your time pointing people to the One True Savior? We have to be careful as Jesus exalts us for His glory and purpose that we continually humble ourselves and point any followers to Jesus alone. It is easy to get caught up in the popularity or excitement of what God is doing, but God is clear about not sharing His throne with another. Maybe this is a good time for us to answer the question, "Are we sitting on any thrones that rightfully belong to Jesus?"

The times that I unknowingly took on the "savior" role in someone's life by trying to always be everything to them, never ended well. Some signs that you are taking on the "savior" role is when a person is coming to you daily or every other day with all their problems and needs. You feel guilty by not being there for them at every turning point. You are spending much of your time and attention on one person, when the rest of your life is sitting on the back burner. You enjoy when people talk about how much you know about God. You allow the comments of, "Now you are here, things are happening and all this good is because of you."

Quick! If you find yourself in this role, step down and bow the knee to the Only One who is able to really save a person - Jesus. Confess to Jesus and to people that you are unable to do any of these things. Give credit where credit is due. Point that person or those people to Jesus and fire yourself as a "false savior." What I have found to be true is anytime you sit on a man-made throne that only belongs to Jesus, it is only a matter of time that you will fall. I am so thankful for spiritual giants like John the Baptist who took no interest in having a following, but instead, pointed others to Jesus - the only One worthy to follow. I'm not saying you shouldn't listen to people when they need someone, but I think we need to be pointing them to Christ as we listen.

As a man of God, John had to take some stands in his life. Just like in our world today, there were people who hated those who followed completely after Jesus. Let's look into scenes from John's ministry. Read Luke 3:1-20.

List some of the people John spoke to and what message he had for them?

What does verse 18-20 say?

Let's get a closer look into the scene between John the Baptist and Herod. Read Matthew 14:1-4.

What sin did John bring to light that landed him in prison?

This is a great time to remind ourselves that John was human with flesh and blood, feelings, fears, and real emotions just like us. Even so, he was still willing to preach the truth and point others to Christ.

Look at Matthew 11:1-5. What did John ask his disciples to ask Jesus?

Growing up in the United States, we are so easily put off or feel persecution as Christians about things that would seem minor to much of the world. Throughout the world many Christians are giving their lives for their faith and trust in Jesus. The Bible is clear that all Christians will undergo trials and persecution in some way for their faith.

I recently spoke with some believers who are serving God faithfully, but growing weary in the persecutions. I asked each person to share their most significant experience of reaching people for the gospel during this time in their lives. Each one had a profound story to tell. Although I wanted them out of the pain of hardship, I told them to focus on the goal, on those who are being saved, and the lives that are being changed for all of eternity.

Do you or someone you know need a fresh reminder that their work in the Lord is not in vain? The focus has to shift from the circumstances to the eternal work that God is doing. What does 1 Corinthians 15:58 say?

We know Jesus hurt when he heard about John the Baptist in prison. He knew of John's future beheading and He had the power to free him. Did Jesus not care? John was one of His own, His friend, the one who spent His life preparing for the coming of Jesus? The one who baptized Jesus and pointed to Him alone? Of course he cared! But Jesus knew there was something greater to be done then stepping in. Just as Jesus knew God Himself would want to step in on His behalf when He would go through His death on the cross. We have to live by faith when the very people we are serving are treating us unfairly or we are being hurt. Our faith will keep us from being offended when we don't see God stepping in on our behalf. Yes, He is able. Yes, He does care and yes, He sees your pain, afflictions, and those who cause them. Not only that, but the enemy knows when he hurts one of God's children, he is hurting the heart of God. But even so, in the pain of it all, a greater glory is to be revealed and many lives are to be brought to salvation.

Therefore, my dear brothers, stand firm. Let nothing move you. Always give yourselves fully to the work of the Lord, because you know that your labor in the Lord is not in vain.

1 Corinthians 15:58

Instead of freeing John, how did Jesus respond to John in Matthew 11:1-6?

Continue to read Matthew 11:7-11 and write out in your own words what Jesus told the listeners about John the Baptist.

Read Matthew 14:5-12

Why was Herod afraid to put John the Baptist to death? (v. 5)

What happened in verse 6-11?

What did the disciples do in verse 12?

Not only did John sit in prison, but He ended up giving up his life for the gospel. Are you willing to trust God even when the season seems to be long and you know it is going to take a death of sorts to bring something back to life in your life? This is when it gets hard. We serve a living God who is eternal. He doesn't look at this life as we do. When we leave this earth, our life is just beginning. The life we now live is just a shadow of what's to come. But our earthly minds have a hard time grasping the mysteries of God.

In these times, we need a lot of time with Jesus, who promises to never leave or forsake us. He promises to heal us completely and to show us His glory. Jesus Himself had to suffer and we, too, will suffer. However, we will also get to bask in His glory as He reveals Himself to us. I believe as we turn to Jesus during our times of suffering and hide in the shadow of His wings, we see Him in ways that other people may never experience.

There is no wasted suffering with Jesus. His thoughts are not our thoughts and His ways are not our ways. They are higher and with a greater purpose than we can see, hear, or conceive with our human minds.

What does Isaiah 43:1-2 tell us?

I read a book called, "10 Who Changed the World", by Daniel Akin written 2012. I was excited when I first picked up this book because there is something exciting about being a part of change, especially changing the world. However, as I read each story, I realized that change and the salvation of others came through the hardships, of these 10 and for some, their death. That's hard for "comfortable Christianity." One thing that stood out was each of these revealed that the people were more concerned about the lost people they wanted to come to know Christ than their own lives. Consider the following excerpt:

> "The Faithfulness of God is the only certain thing in the world today. We need not fear the result of trusting Him. Those words were penned by John Tam, a young missionary to China, who along with his gifted wife Betty would trust King Jesus all the way to their beheading. They would accept the sovereign results of God in their lives, which came to an untimely end at the tender ages of twenty-eight (Betty) and twenty-seven (John). Missionary Daniel Smith noted: 'They were roughly handled, stripped of their outward clothing, painfully bound, and publicly beheaded. They died – but not without the comfort and support of the Lord, and not without the light of life shining through the darkest circumstances life could bring."[1]

We've heard more and more of the beheadings of believers for their faith. When I think of Hebrews 11, I think of those who have gone before us and persevered by faith, even to death. Revelation is prophecy to come. What does Revelation 20:4 say?

In 10 who changed the world,

> Jim Elliot saw our God for who he is and a holy reverence and fear attended him while at Wheaton and drove him to take the gospel to the Aucas," an unreached people group. "Jim Elliot wrote in a letter to his family: 'Remember you are immortal until your work is done. But don't let the sand of time get into the eyes of your vision to reach those who still sit in darkness. They simply must hear.' Just before he left for the last time, Elizabeth (his wife) asked Jim if they [Jim and the other men] were attacked by the Aucas, would they use their guns? Jim's response was clear and certain: 'We will not use our guns!' When Elizabeth asked why, he simply said, 'Because we are ready for heaven, but they are not.'" He and four others did die by the hand of those they were sharing the gospel with. However, the ones who took their lives did come to know Christ as Lord and Savior in the years after their death. Matthew 10:28 says, "Do not be afraid of those who kill the body but cannot kill the soul. Rather, be afraid of the One who can destroy both soul and body in hell.[2]

I sat there after reading each story that weekend and thought, "I'm so comfortable. This just doesn't seem right." Within a couple of weeks my comfortable world was rocked and the months to follow would be anything but comfortable. I look back on that season and see how being uncomfortable was bringing about God's purposes and glory. Our God is unlike any other and He can be trusted. When the cloud seems to be so thick and you are unable to see from all the fog, remember who holds it all in His hands. Maybe we just need to be reminded that our God, Maker of heaven and earth loves us so much that He, too, went through the suffering of sending His son, Jesus. And He experienced what it was to suffer for the sake of a greater heavenly calling, for you and for me. Jesus gave his very own life and He was beaten and mocked and nailed to an old rugged cross taking on divine wrath for all of our sins. It was by the cross that God brought salvation to the world. We, too, will die the first death, but Jesus went before us so we would not have to die the second. Because of His death, we live forever.

God really does love you and me. Read John 3:16

Let's be reminded of our key scripture and fill in the blanks.

"I consider that our present _____ are not _____ comparing with

the _____ that will be revealed to us" (Romans 8:18).

Notes

1. Akin, Daniel L. *10 Who Changed the World.* (Nashville, TN: B&H Books, 2012), 139.
2. Ibid, 81.

Week 6

VICTORY IN JESUS

Love your neighbor

"You shall love the LORD your God with all your heart, with all your soul, with all your strength, and with all your mind, and love your neighbor as yourself." ~ Luke 10:27

I hope you are excited and ready for our final week of homework. Recently, I've heard a song by Chris Tomlin, entitled, "Your Heart." The chorus says, "At the end of the day, I wanna hear people say My heart looks like Your heart, My heart looks like Your heart. When the world looks at me, let them agree, that My heart looks like Your heart, My heart looks like Your heart." My desire is by the end of this study our hearts look more like Jesus' heart.

Today, let's stare into the love Jesus has for us. What does Matthew 1:21 say why they were to name Him Jesus?

The name Jesus means, "The LORD saves." What does Luke 19:10 say Jesus came to do?

Jesus' whole existence on the earth was to come and save us from our sins. "For God so loved the world that He gave his one and only son that whoever believes in Him shall not perish but have everlasting life" (John 3:16). What does John 17:3 say eternal life is?

Jesus came to save you and me because of His love for us. Before Jesus came, God's people were following the law that had been passed down from Moses. However, even though the law revealed sin and where we fall short, it never made anyone righteous.

I want us to take a look at what Paul wrote to the Corinthians in 1 Corinthian 13. Paul came from a Pharisee background. At an early age he memorized the Torah and spent his life living according to the law and teaching others to do so as well. However, there was a problem. Before Paul's conversion from Saul, he did not have a relationship with Christ. He even went as far as persecuting Christians because he believed they were going against the law. After Paul received Christ, he realized it was no longer about the law, but about Jesus. In 1 Corinthians 13 he gives the church of Corinth the key to everything we do. What is the key?

What does it say

If I speak in tongues of men and of angels, **but have not love**, _____

_____" (1 Corinthians 13:1).

If I have the gift of prophecy and can fathom all mysteries and all knowledge, and if I have a faith that can move mountains, **but have not love**, _____

_____" (1 Corinthians 13:2).

If I give all I possess to the poor and surrender my body to the flames, **but have not love**, _____

_____"

(1 Corinthians 13:3).

Each one of these examples hit the extremes: to be able to speak with the tongue of angels, to be able to fathom all mysteries, knowledge, and have enough faith to move the mountains, and to even go as far in your obedience to surrender your body to the flames. Wouldn't you think that would count for something? But as we can see from our answers above, without love we only sound like noise, we are nothing and we gain nothing. A lost and dying world is looking for love, longing for someone to care.

What does 1 Corinthians 13:4-8 say love is?

These people honor me with their lips, but their hearts are far from me. They worship me in vain; their teachings are but rules taught by men." Matthew 15:8-9

1 Corinthians 13 reminds us how vital love is in everything we do.

This reminds me of what Jesus said to the Pharisees and teachers of the law in Matthew 15:8-9. Read the verses in the margin and fill in the blanks below.

These people honor me with their _____, but their _____ are far

from me. They _____ me in _____; their teachings are but

_____ taught by _____.

Jesus consistently showed compassion for the people around Him. However, the way He showed compassion changed according to the situation. Complete the following table to see how Jesus demonstrated His compassion.

Verse	How did Jesus showed compassion?
Matthew 14:14	
Matthew 15:32, 35-37	
Matthew 20:34	
Mark 6:34, 42	
Luke 7: 13-15	

We have to know that our love for God and our love for our neighbor comes from God's love for us.

"We love because He first loved us" (1 John 4:19).

Open up to Luke 10 and begin reading verses 25-29.

Who is talking to Jesus? (v. 25)

Why does he question Jesus? (v. 25)

According to verse 27, We are to love the Lord our God with...

All our_____   All our_____

All our_____   All our_____

And how are we to love our neighbor?

"But he wanted to justify himself, so he asked Jesus, 'And who is my neighbor?'" The lawyer was not focused on the love of God or his neighbor, but the law and his own self-righteousness based on the law" (Luke 10:29).

Let's continue to read in Luke to see how Jesus responded to this export in the law. Read Luke 10:30.

Where was the man traveling from and to?

The man fell among thieves. What did they do to this man?

Read verses 31 and 32. What two men saw this man wounded and half dead?

Two men who would have been coming from Jerusalem, a priest, and a Levite who assist Priests in the work of the temple. Jerusalem was the place of worship, so both of these men may have just left a time of worship.

What action did each take?

Priest: _____   Levite: _____

The expert of the law could most likely identify with these two people. The priest and the Levite would have known the law and even taught the law to others. Sometimes we are so caught up in ourselves, our thoughts and our plans, we cannot see the thoughts and plans God has for us right in front of us. This man who was beaten and left for dead would have required much of the person who decided to stop and care for him.

Why do you think the Levite and the Priest passed the man by?

By showing us the Priest and the Levite, Jesus was revealing to the expert of the law, you cannot do this from your own righteousness. Even those who this man and others would have seemed to be the most righteous, cannot be righteous enough on their own.

There is no one righteous, not even one.

Romans 3:10

What does Romans 3:10 say?

Now read Luke 10:33 and name the next man who passed by.

The Bible says that the Samaritan saw him as he journeyed. Before we go on, let's be reminded of a few things. First, the Samaritan was despised by the Jews therefore he didn't stop because this man was a friend or even liked him. Also, the Samaritan had things to do. We know this in later verses because he takes him to the inn and pays for his care while he is gone, but comes back for him. You and I have things to do; work, kids, a home to take care of and other responsibilities.

The Samaritan didn't allow his daily work to keep him from helping this man. Instead, when the Samaritan saw the man "he had _____." (see Luke 10:33). What better way to preach the gospel.

Jesus never taught anything that He himself wasn't already doing. Every time it says, Jesus was moved with compassion, it shows He moved into action. The Greek word for compassion in Luke 10:33, that the Samaritan had, is the same word used when Jesus was moved with compassion: "**splagchnizomai; meaning to be moved in the inward parts.**"1 When was the last time you saw someone and you were moved to the point that you did something about it?

Continue reading Luke 10:34-37 What are the six things the Samaritan did for the man? (Verse 34).

What did the Samaritan do in verse 35?

Who did the lawyer answer was his neighbor?

When the lawyer identified who the neighbor was, what did Jesus tell him to do? (v. 37)

In order for us to have a heart like Jesus, we must follow His example.

We attended a Centrifuge camp one summer with a group of students. I remember toward the end of the week they took us into the large auditorium and announced to the entire group that we would go in our small groups to complete a scavenger hunt and whoever returned first was the winner. I'm not by nature a competitive person, but I found myself wanting to win on this particular night. I was a part of the adult leader group.

When they said go, we were to go from place to place and complete a task, directed by a staffer and move to the next place. As we got in line to receive our first item from a staffer, the staffer continued to detain us by asking about the gospel, speaking with a foreign accent. All I could think was, "She is trying to make us run behind and we need to hurry up." Finally, we received what we needed to proceed to the next location. We ran as fast as we could and when we arrived, we were met by another staffer who was less interested in giving us what we needed, and more interested in asking us questions about the gospel, putting us behind in winning our game.

After we left the second person, we stopped and looked at one another. Maybe the goal is not to be first, but to share the gospel as we go. We headed back to the first person and began sharing the gospel. By the time all groups were back and seated, a video began playing on the screen. One by one other staffers, who had not been a part of the scavenger hunt got up to the microphone and began sharing how groups passed them by during the game. The video on the screen showed one of the staffers carrying 3 large boxes and as we watch the video, we hear, "300 of you passed me by and not one offered to help." The next staffer we see on the video with his car hood popped and he is by the car, "5 groups walked right by me and no one offered to help." The next staffer was posed as someone who was homeless, and she said, "200 of you walked by and no one took time to notice." As soon as each spoke, the video showed a woman on the streets of New York, sitting, rocking back and forth, by a shopping cart and people literary walking over her without stopping. Talk about feeling small. All week we were in worship and Bible study, away from everyday life, with the perfect opportunity to help. But, each one of us, when given a goal, left that building only focusing on our goal, forgetting that our real goal, every day is to share the gospel and love our neighbor, wherever that may be.

The good Samaritan is a word picture of our Savior. Jesus saw us in our depravity of sin and knew we were left for dead because of our sin. Just as Isaiah prophesied, he would be rejected by men, a man of many sorrows and acquainted with grief on our behalf. He left His place in heaven. He didn't pass us by, but as Psalm 147:3 says, "He heals the brokenhearted and binds up their wounds." He left the deposit of the Holy Spirit with us and will one day come back for us. Just like in the story of the Samaritan, Jesus paid it all. Take a look at John 15:5-17.

What must we do to bear much fruit? (v. 5)

What brings God much glory? (v. 8)

Write a summary of verse 9-17 in your own words?

In John 13:34-35 and John 15:16-17 Jesus is preparing His disciples for His departure. What is the command He gives them in both of these passages?

John 15:16-17

John 13:34-35

Let us conclude with our key scripture today

"You shall _____ the LORD your God with all your _____, with all your

_____, with all your _____, and with all your _____, and love your

_____ as yourself" (Luke 10:27).

A new command I give you: Love one another. As I have loved you, so you must love one another. John 13:34-35

Arise and Go

"Go therefore and make disciples of all the nations, baptizing them in the name of the Father and of the Son and of the Holy Spirit, teaching them to observe all things that I have commanded you; and lo, I am with you always, even to the end of the age." Matthew 28:19-20

Yesterday, we learned who Jesus says is our neighbor and as we begin today's lesson, I want us to be reminded of the last words spoken between Jesus and the expert of the law. Luke 10:36-37 says, "So which of these three do you think was neighbor to him who fell among the thieves?" And he said, "He who showed mercy on him." Then Jesus said to him, "Go and do likewise."

Read Matthew 28:18-20

What command does Jesus give to his disciples in verse 19? _____

The same word go in Luke 10:37 is the same word Jesus uses here. Guess what the meaning is? Go! I hope today's lesson excites you and moves you into action. However, before we move into action, I want us to go back to Luke 10 and look at the passage that comes directly after the Samaritin. Open and read Luke 10:38-42

Describe under each person's name what they were doing when Jesus was in their house?

MARY (see Luke 10:39)

MARTHA (see Luke 10:38, 40)

How does Luke 10:40 describe Martha's state of mind?

The word for distracted in the Greek is perispao, "to draw around, to draw away, to be driven about mentally, to be over-occupied, too busy, about a thing."2

My kids know when someone is coming over. The air seems to thicken as I rush around, distracted about the details. There is always a meal to prepare and cleaning to be accomplished. I find myself at

But one thing is needed, and Mary has chosen that good part, which will not be taken away from her (Luke 10:42, NKJV)

times fussing at my family because I'm not enjoying the preparation, but as my commentary says about Martha, I am "fussing about with details that are unnecessarily elaborate."

What did Martha say to Jesus in Luke 10:40?

Let's look at Jesus' answer in the next two verses. First, what did he say to Martha in verse 41?

And what three things did Jesus say to Martha in verse 42?

1.

2.

3.

I want us to stare at what Mary had chosen, "the good part" (see Luke 10:42). "The Greek word here for good is agathos, meaning intrisically good. Agathos is defined as what originates from God and is empowered by Him in their life, through faith."3 The key to agathos is it originates from God alone. What does Luke 18:19 say about the good in us?

The same Greek word for good is used here. Jesus was saying only God was good. Read Matthew 1:23 and write the name that would be given to Jesus and the meaning of that name?

Let's pull all this together. Jesus was stating in Luke 18:19 and Luke 10:42, He is the good part. As in the beginning of today's lesson, we are called to go, to serve, to share the good news of Jesus Christ. However, we first have to sit and receive the Word, the good part. As we sit with Jesus, we receive the good. It is in receiving God's Word, we are empowered by Him in our lives, through faith, to go and do what He has commanded us to do. If we try to go without receiving His Word, we will serve and use our gifts, but we will find ourselves as Martha. A state of being distracted and troubled by many things, missing out on the most important thing, Jesus.

The Word of God has a way of empowering us to do as Jesus commanded us to do, "Go." We need to go in the power of Jesus, having compassion and mercy that we spoke about in yesterday's lesson. A believer who has heard the Word, and goes by faith will receive God's power to do amazing things for His Glory.

Let me give you an example of my own life. I can recall the first time I ever served at a food kitchen for the homeless. My husband and I took a youth group from the small town in which we lived, to down town St. Louis. When we arrived the first evening, fear gripped me and many of the students. We watched from windows as people arrived to receive an evening meal. Several of our students went down to the cafeteria and came up overwhelmed with fear and judgement. I knew if something didn't change, our trip would not be successful. That night we had a worship service for our students and my husband preached the Word. As soon as the Word was spoken, our hearts began to change. Throughout the night, as we prayed, the fear left, and a Spirit of courage, love, mercy and compassion came over our entire group. The next day was so amazing. Our students were not only serving, but fellowshiping and enjoying their time with all the people.

I personally got to be a part of a survey trying to help better serve the homeless of St. Louis. As people told their stories, I realized they were no different than me. At one point, I looked over and saw my son Bryce, who was three at the time, asking a homeless man for chips that the man had bought himself at the local convenient store. He freely shared his chips with Bryce. I thought to myself, "I am so humbled at this man's generousity." I also thought, "I look around and see "homeless people" and my kids, Bryce 3, and Alexis 8, (at the time), just see "people."

Write out a time in your life where you went in your own strength and failed, but later sat with Jesus and felt empowered to do what you were originally unable to do.

Now that we know we must spend time with Jesus first, I would like us to spend the remainder of this lesson on the command to "Go" by looking at some more scriptures.

We know Paul as the man who wrote 13 books of the Bible and preached the gospel to the Gentiles. But, do you know the disciple Ananias? Let's begin our journey of "Go" by reading Acts 9:1-20..

Let's trail the series of events...Saul thought he was serving God by persecuting Christians. What was Saul doing in verses 1-5 and what happened to him on the Damascus road?

God came to Saul while he was in the middle of breathing threats and murder and preparing for more persecution to Christians. What did Jesus respond to Saul's question, "Lord, what do You want me to do" in Acts 9:6?

Look back at verse 10. There was a certain disciple. What is his name?

How did God speak to him? (v. 10)

How did Ananias respond? (v. 10)

What command did God give to Ananias? (v. 11)

How did Ananias respond? (v. 13,14)

How did God respond to Ananias? (verse 15,16)

What did Ananias do? (verse 17)

What was the result of his obedience? (verse 18)

As a result of Ananias' faith and obedience to "Go", Saul heard the Word and became a believer. What happened in verse 19?

What did Saul do in verse 20?

Do you see how God was the One who prepared the Way? He had already prepared Saul to receive the Word spoken by Ananias. God could have used anyone, but chose to use Ananias. One person's obedience really matters. I cannot help but think of the Butterfly Effect, by Andy Andrews. He says, "There are generations yet unborn, whose very lives will be shifted and shaped by the moves you make and the actions you take"4 - especially when you know that your actions are a direct result of what God has told you to do. After Saul's conversion, he became known as Paul. Paul not only became the first missionary preaching the gospel to the Gentiles which affects you and me today, he also wrote 13 books of the Bible. Ananias had a part in all of that by being a part of Paul's conversion.

Paul went on to mentor young Timothy. What did he tell Timothy in 2 Timothy 4:2?

We, too, are to be prepared to preach the word in season and out of season. I want to give you a couple of examples from my own life about being prepared in season and out of season.

In Season

A couple of years ago, my husband and I took a youth group to a mission's camp. Our group was able to go into the city and witness in a housing neighborhood. There was a group of Christians who would weekly go to this place, so the people were not completely taken off guard by our arrival. Our students had previously experienced several opportunities to serve people in this kind of setting, so I believe they were prepared. Our group was large so we divided up among two different places. When we arrived at our location, I asked the Lord, "What purpose do you want us to serve?" The first day we made animal balloons, face painted, and used other activities to bring kids out. As the kids came out, we played and talked with them. Many of them seemed skeptical of us. I'm sure everything about us looked vastly different. After the activities, the kids sat in a large group so we could sing and share the gospel. Because it was a large group, it was really hard to understand what was being said. I left that day thinking, "The purpose must be to show these kids love."

To my surprise, God showed up in an unexpected way on the second day. One of our guides gave us sidewalk chalk to add to our activities. I observed a small boy drawing with the chalk with one of our students. She asked the young boy, "Is that a cross?" pointing to his drawing of a lowercase "t." He replied, "No, it's a "t" in my name." God used that one small stroke of a lowercase "t" and that student who was looking for her opportunity to share Jesus to change the whole atmosphere. She began to tell the young boy about Jesus through sidewalk chalk. One by one we all took notice and began sharing the gospel to kids by taking sidewalk chalk and sharing stories from the Bible. I shared the story of salvation with a young girl sitting next to me. But an older girl listened as I shared the message. When the little girl got up, the older girl moved closer to me. I shared with her about salvation and she said she wanted to give her life to Jesus. I gave her the gospel as clearly as I knew how and she prayed to Jesus asking him to save her. When we looked up from our prayer, another girl said she wanted to hear what I was sharing and she also accepted Christ that day.

The next day would be our last and I wanted to bring both these girls a Bible and a devotion; however, being so early in the morning, I didn't see anything open on our way to the neighborhood except a Kroger. I went in and found exactly two Bibles and two small books for girls containing 365 days of devotion. I couldn't wait to show the girls their Bibles and how to look up scripture for themselves. When I finally had the opportunity to sit with them, I began showing them how to find scripture. When they opened to that day's date, the devotion was on Philip and the Ethiopian in Acts 8:26-40.

What Word was spoke to Philip? (v. 26)

What did Philip do? (v. 27)

As he started out, what did Philip see? (vs. 27-28)

What did Philip hear in verse 29?

As we see in the rest of the passage, Philip witnessed to the Ethiopian eunuch, who God was preparing to listen to Philip's message.

I sat there in amazement at the exact devotion, the exact date, and the devotion was an exact Word for these girls.

Out of Season

While I was writing this study, our family moved to a neighborhood with many kids. In preparation for week six, I concentrated my reading in the books of the gospels. As I began reading something interesting happened. Instead of writing, my eyes and heart were open to those around me and one by one, I took every opportunity God gave me to share Jesus' love and life with my neighbors. One particular day, several kids were on my front porch and I felt the Holy Spirit leading me to ask them to come over for a Bible study and then swim. I'd been wanting to share the gospel with the kids, but I found myself on this day making excuses. I thought, "I could use that time to write." In my spirit I heard, "Do you want to write about it or live it?" Enough said. I asked the kids to come swim and told them we would do a short Bible study before we got into the pool. All the kids were excited. That night I shared the gospel with several kids. A couple of the kids gave their own testimony of salvation and a couple of the kids said, "We are not saved yet."

The next morning as I was having my quiet time two kids knocked on my door. I went to the door and told them my kids were still in bed. After I closed the door, they sat down on my porch. Sitting in my living room it occurred to me to invite them in for morning Bible study with my kids. I woke up my family and invited the kids to have Bible study with us. They excitedly joined us. My two youngest children gave their testimonies and I shared the gospel with our young neighbors.

The Lord is teaching me what it looks like to be ready in season and out of season. To do this, I must be willing to follow Mary's example to sit at Jesus' feet and learn from Him. As we end today's lesson, I encourage you to spend time in prayer seeking God's guidance to plan time in your day to sit at His feet to prepare to share the gospel as the opportunity arises.

Finish today's lesson by looking back at what Jesus commands us to do and fill in the blanks.

"_____ therefore and _____ disciples of all the _____, baptizing them in the

name of the Father and of the Son and of the Holy Spirit, _____ them to observe

_____ things that I have _____ you; and lo, _____ am with you

_____, even to the end of the age" (Matthew 28:19-20).

Do you believe

"But without faith it is impossible to please Him, for he who comes to God must believe that He is, and that He is a rewarder of those who diligently seek Him." ~ Hebrews 11:6 NKJV

Today, as I share with you my personal testimony of God's healing in my son's life, we will also go to the book of Mark to observe the power of Jesus Christ in the lives of a man and woman who experienced the healing power of Jesus.

When my son Bryce was nine months old we learned he had severe allergies to corn, wheat, soy, milk, peanuts, celery, and eggs. We also learned the compounding effects of his medical condition. For example, Bryce's growth was affected by his lack of nutrition. Additionally, as he aged, he was able to stand with support, but his ability to walk was delayed. Because Bryce couldn't walk, he crawled everywhere. This was especially troubling in the church nursery where he would sometimes eat crumbs of other children's snacks, which led to allergic reactions and trips to the emergency room.

Let's pause my story for a moment to look at Mark 5 and follow Jairus and the woman who was bleeding for 12 years as they come to Jesus. Read Mark 5:21-43

How many people were around when Jarius approached Jesus? (Verse 21)

Who was Jarius? (Verse 22)

According to verses 22-23, what did Jairus do and say when he saw Jesus?

What does verse 24 say Jesus did?

We are told in Mark 5:42, Jairus' daughter was 12 years old. She was dying. Before we move forward, I want you to think this through. Although he was a ruler within the synagogue, his position was unable to affect his daughter's impending death.

Jarius was facing the death of his beloved daughter. Perhaps you are also facing a difficult situation. If so, list it here.

If your only hope is a miracle, today's lesson is for you.

In verse 25 we learn Jarius did not have to go home alone, but Jesus went with him. This story reminds us that although we may have to go through hard times before we receive complete healing, God walks with us on this journey so we can know Him more.

Now let's pick up with my story to catch a few glimpses of Jesus' presence along the way with me. One Sunday morning Bryce had to have a breathing treatment before church. As I sat there with him, I pulled out my Bible and read. Later that day, after the Sunday evening worship service, we picked Bryce up from the church nursery. By the time we got home, he was having difficulty breathing, so we got back in the car to head to the emergency room. Because his breathing seemed so poor, I unbuckled him from his car seat to hold him. The hospital was close by and when we got close enough to see the ER, a car pulled out in front of us. I remember vividly putting one hand on the back of Bryce's head and the other on his back, (slowly going with a quick movement forward and then back, never taking my hand off). Although we were okay, the man in the other car ended up on a stretcher. While my husband stayed with the man and the responders, I walked the rest of the way to the ER, holding Bryce in my arms.

After we got home, I went back to the same place where I was that morning, for another breathing treatment with Bryce. My Bible was still in the same spot opened. I could not believe my eyes when I looked down at my Bible. It was opened to Psalm 91 and my eyes looked right at verses 11-12. Take a look for yourself.

For He will command His angels concerning you to guard you in all your ways; they will lift you up in their hands, so you will not strike your foot against a stone.
Psalm 91:11-12 N

In your own life, how has God shown you that He is walking with you through your present trial of faith?

Just as God was with you, He was with Jairus, and He was about to show Jairus His power in another person's need before He made it to his house. Continue reading Mark 5:24-34.

Who was in the crowd that day? And what was her need? (verse 25)

According to Mark 5:26 what actions had she taken to address her need and what had been the result?

I don't believe the woman suffered for 12 years for no reason. Jesus was about to perform a miracle. When He performs a miracle He wants everyone to know it is truly a miracle. She had been to doctor after doctor. She didn't just bleed for a few days, but day after day for 12 years. Her physical, mental, and spiritual energy was drained. Everyone could see she had tried everything and nothing was working. This miracle was not just for her, but for the crowd, her family, Jairus, you, and me.

What does Mark 5:27 say the woman did?

What does verse 28 say the woman thought?

Take a look at 2 Corinthians 4:13 in the margin and fill in the blanks below.

It is written: "I _____; therefore ___ have _____." With that same

spirit of _____, we also _____ and therefore _____.

It is written: "I believed therefore I have spoken." With that same spirit of faith we also believe and therefore speak. 2 Corinthians 4:13

Read Mark 5:29-32. How long did it take from the time the woman touched Jesus' cloak for the woman to stop bleeding and experience healing?

Besides the woman, who else noticed was she was healed? (verse 30)

This is a great time to recognize that Jairus, who needed Jesus to heal his young daughter, had not received his miracle yet. However, he continued believing as He walked with Jesus to his house. We see two people - the woman and Jairus. The woman received instant healing, and the other had a journey with Jesus before he sees the healing. Probably we would choose immediate healing. However, when your healing takes time you find yourself walking closely with Jesus. Every step is a step of faith. You travel with him in really hard places having to continue to state your faith in Jesus, every step of the way. When the day arrives when he answers your prayer, you gained much more than healing. You gain a gift of deep- rooted trust and intimacy with Jesus that no one can take from you.

What does Mark 5:33 say the woman did right in front of the crowd, the disciples, and Jesus?

She confessed what Jesus had done for her. Right there in the middle of a crowd, with the disciples around. What does verse 33 say about the woman's emotional state when she fell down before Jesus?

She mustered up the strength to come and confess, even while fearful and trembling. She didn't wait until she got her composure or was strengthened in faith. Jesus asked in verse 31, "Who touched Me?" She didn't have time to get it together. She just had to obey. I could ask myself the same question I am about to ask you. What are you waiting on to obey Jesus fully?

Sometimes we don't get to go and "get it together" but we have to take the faith we've been given and go even if we are fearing and trembling.

Jairus was also watching this unfold. What array of thoughts do you think Jairus was experiencing at this time?

I believe what happened to the woman must had been building Jairus' faith. On the other hand he might have been too distracted by his own circumstances to see this healing as an opportunity to build his faith.

The woman had no way of knowing what her faith was accomplishing in Jairus' heart. Likewise, we have to be obedient to what God calls us to do and know God will use our faith and obedience in the lives of those around us.

Before we move on to Jairus' house, let's read Mark 5:34.

How did Jesus address this certain woman in the crowd?

What did He say made her well?

What other two things did He tell her in verse 34?

To the crowd, she was just a "certain woman." To Jesus, she was His daughter. You may feel unnoticed, unloved, just a person in the crowd; but, Jesus names you as His when you put your faith and trust in Him. He healed her and sent her away in peace. Not only is the affliction healed, but the anxiety that comes with the days, months, or years of affliction. Jesus says, "Go in _____" (Mark 5:34).

What other test does Jarius experience in Mark 5:35?

Jesus had just said, "Daughter, your faith has made you well." And then Jairus hears that his daughter is dead. Jairus hears those words that the enemy loves to speak to us, "Why trouble the Teacher any further."

When was the last time you thought, "Okay, I'm believing" and you confess your faith. Then you hear more bad news and in your mind you hear, "Give up. No need in believing anymore." Just like with Jairus these words can come from those closest to you and even from those who should be encouraging you the most.

One morning as I sat in the hospital under an oxygen tent with Bryce, I opened up my Bible and began reading the 23rd Psalm. After my reading, I cried to the Lord and expressed my trust in Him. Before I was even finished with my reading and journaling, the dietitian came in and stated several things that were hard to hear. Because I am trained as a Registered Dietitian, this hit me really hard. I could hear the enemy taunting me, "You are a dietitian and cannot even keep your son from being malnourished. You cannot even figure out all these food allergies." I am reminded of Jesus, our Savior when he was on the cross. What words did the chief priests, scribes, and elders say to Jesus, mocking him in Matthew 27:41-42?

After the dietitian left, Bryce's doctor came in and as she spoke, I heard words of doubt, fear, and unbelief. However, immediately after she left, I opened my Bible and read from Mark. Continue reading Mark 5:35-40.

What did Jesus immediately speak to Jairus? (verse36)

Don't be afraid _____ (your name). Just believe!

At this point, Jairus had a choice to make. He could give up at the advice of his friends or choose to trust Jesus. Verse 37 tells us that Jairus chose to continue to trust Jesus.

Who did Jesus allow to go with him to Jairus' house? (verse 37)

What did Jesus do with the crowd at Jairus' house? (verse 40)

In Bryce's hospital room, I read those words and the Lord spoke to me in my spirit and said, "Put all the unbelieving thoughts out of your mind." I didn't see any miracle on that day, but what I did receive was a renewed faith that Jesus was in control.

When God gives us a specific Word about something He is going to do we must be careful to guard the thoughts that come into our mind.

During the course of Bryce's illness, I had been leading a small prayer group and I felt led to lead my first ever Bible study, Believing God, by Beth Moore. I knew I needed it as much as the ladies who would go through the study with me. Having all the videos in hand, I decided to wake up at 6:00 every morning and watch a video. One morning, I finished watching the video and I heard in my spirit, "Do you believe I healed Bryce?" Several times that morning I heard those same words in my spirit. I knew if I gave Bryce a cracker believing He was healed, and he wasn't, I would have harm my son and have to rush him to the ER.

Later that morning, I was at the sink doing dishes and the story of Abraham and Isaac came to my mind. Abraham believed God to the point he was willing to harm his son. Let me interject, Abraham knew human sacrifice was not what God wanted, but he knew if God took his son, he would raise him from the dead. I thought to myself, if I give Bryce a cracker, I will harm him. About an hour later, I sat down to prepare for our Women on Mission meeting we were having that evening. I had the bundle of Mosiac Magazines still in the plastic wrap they came in. I opened the magazine. Right there was the story of Abraham and Isaac. I just knew. I knew God was speaking to me and I had to obey. I had never witnessed a physical healing, like I had begged God for throughout the past year, but I was filled with faith by His word. Even though my flesh was weak, I gave Bryce a cracker and stated the truths I was learning in my Bible study. I chose to believe God's specific Word to me. This was not a name it and claim it moment. This was my choice to step out in faith, believing God had healed my son. And guess what? Bryce was healed!!! Listen to that again. Bryce was healed. Just like the woman who had bled for 12 years, I confessed to my husband with fear and trembling what God had done. That afternoon we tried other foods that he couldn't eat just the day before. Again he did not react. We were amazed and little by little introduced foods to him of each category. We saw some complete healing of foods overnight, but as far as his overall health, it was six months to be restored. I had experienced, like the woman, immediate healing by the power of Jesus according to faith. Like Jairus, I had seen Jesus reveal himself over the course of our journey. I'd like to say that was the end of the story with Bryce's healing. Unfortunately, there is more to the story. Although I was willing to introduce most of the foods he was allergic to, I did not offer him peanut butter. Thinking back now, for all the faith I had there was still an element of doubt. I chose not to offer him the peanut butter and later learned this was the one allergy that remained.

Returning to our story in Mark. Read Mark 5:41-43

How did it turn out for Jairus?

Jairus did not have to prove what Jesus did for his daughter. It was obvious to all those who had been watching his daughter through her sickness and her death. They witnessed the journey and was able to physically see and hear the miracle themselves.

Many times, when people ask me if Bryce outgrew his allergies, I would say, "No, one day he was not able to have the food, and the next day he was. Jesus performed a miracle in our lives."

I love what the blind man who Jesus healed said, "...One thing I do know, I was blind but now I see" (John 9:25).

For me, my husband, Bryce and all of those around us, we had to go for over a year with such drama, before seeing this miracle. I believe this is because as people, we want to somehow discount the miracle of Jesus Christ and Jesus likes to make sure everyone knows how severe and how hopeless the situation is without Him. So when it happens, there is no doubt that Jesus performed a miracle.

Read Psalm 103:1-5 and list all the benefits we receive from Christ according to this passage.

I also want us to remember that we don't understand why sometimes our healing is complete here on earth and why other times we are believing and have to wait until we get to heaven to see complete healing and to understand the fullness of each circumstance and outcome. The question however, is not whether God is able, but do you believe and will you continue to believe no matter what?

I have a friend whose daughter recently died unexpectanly. She said what God comforts her with is, "We only see a little piece of a much bigger eternal picture. 'Therefore we do not lose heart. Though outwardly we are wasting away, yet inwardly we are being renewed day by day. For our light and momentary troubles are achieving for us an eternal glory that far outweighs them all. So we fixed our eyes not on what is seen, but on what is unseen, since what is seen is temporary, but what is unseen is eternal.'" 2 Corinthians 4:16-16

Look at our key scripture today and fill in the blanks

"But _____ _____ it is _____ to please _____, for he who

comes to God _____ _____ that He _____, and that He is a rewarder of

those who _____ seek _____" (Hebrews 11:6).

Beauty for Ashes

"To console those who mourn in Zion, To give them beauty for ashes, The oil of joy for mourning, the garment of praise for the spirit of heaviness; That they may be called trees of righteousness, The planting of the LORD, that He may be glorified." ~ Isaiah 61:3 NKJV

Come along with me in today's lesson as we see how God fulfilled the prophecy of Isaiah. Isaiah 61:1 begins by saying, "The Spirit of the Sovereign LORD is on me, because the LORD has anointed me to…" Continue reading verses 1-3 and complete the chart to see how God transformed lives and bring beauty from ashes.

Christ	To whom or instead of
Preach the good news	
Bind up	
Proclaim freedom	
Release from darkness	
To comfort	
Provide for	
Bestow a crown of beauty	
Oil of gladness	
Garment of praise	

Take a look at the list and think about your own life. Which one means the most to you and why?

What does Isaiah 61:4 say?

What a glorious scene! In verses 1-3, Isaiah prophesied that Jesus would come and not only would he replace our broken hearts, hurts, darkness, despair, ashes, mourning, and poverty with salvation, healing, freedom, favor, comfort, gladness, praise, and beauty, He goes on a step farther to use our life to "rebuild ruins, restore the places long devastated, and renew ruined cities that have been devastated for generations" (Isaiah 61:4).

Read Luke 4:16-21 and describe what is happening in this scripture.

Jesus tells them that the scripture they know so well and have longed to see is being fulfilled right in front of their eyes and He is the One fulfilling it.

We all have broken places that need healing. What does 2 Corinthians 1:4 say about why God comforts us?

Read John 4:4-15 to learn how Jesus healed a woman's brokenness and brought beauty from ashes.

Where was Jesus?

Here is Jesus, the Son of God, the gift of Salvation and He is at the well. Since we know He is the Son of God and knows everything, let's find out why He was at the well on that day, at that time. Who also came to the well? (v.7)

What did Jesus do in verse 7 that surprised the Samaritan woman?

What did the Samaritan woman say to Him? (v. 9)

In your own words describe the conversation between the woman and Jesus in verses 10-15.

Read John 4:16-18. What did Jesus reveal to her?

Continue reading John 4:25-41

What did the Samaritan woman know about in verse 25?

How did Jesus respond in verse 26?

What did she do? (vs. 28-29)?

This same woman who wouldn't even go with the other women to the well is now running into town proclaiming the good news of Jesus Christ. What happened when she gave her testimony in verse 39?

What happened the next two days according to verses 41-42?

The people were drawn because one woman who encountered Jesus was willing to share her testimony. But once they heard, they drew near to Jesus and believed because of the Word of God. Just as with the Samaritan woman, Jesus takes our brokenness of sin, and trades it in for beauty of the gospel for all who will believe. Salvation is a gift from God.

Her story is our story. Jesus comes to us to reveal to us who He is and who we are. He does not come to condemn us, but to show us our need for salvation. "We have all sinned and fallen short of the glory of God" (Romans 3:23). Jesus came for sinners, regardless of their credentials, health, credit score, age, wealth, or past decisions. Our failures that result from our sinful nature can be redeemed for His glory.

Through Him, we can be witnesses if we are willing to surrender ourselves to Him just like the Samaritan woman did.

Let's take a look at Mark 2:13-17 to see another example of Jesus' transforming power.

Who did Jesus call to follow Him? (vs. 13-14)

Another name for Levi was Matthew. What was Matthew's occupation at the time of his calling? (v. 14)

Tax collectors were despised by the Jews because of their reputation for cheating and supporting Rome. Who else was eating with Jesus in the home of this despised tax collector? (v. 15)

What question did the Pharisees ask Jesus' disciples? (v.16)

Who responded to their question? And what did he say? (v. 17)

I think it is interesting Jesus said these words. As stated above, Romans 3:23 says, "for all have sinned and fall short of the glory of God." And "there is no one righteous, not even one" (Romans 3:10). But what the Pharisees needed to hear and maybe we need to hear is that we have to recognize we are sinners in order to be saved. We are fooling ourselves when we think we have any righteousness on our own. "It is only by grace that we are saved through faith. It is a gift of God, so no man can boast" (Ephesians 2:8-9). That is why the news of the gospel is so beautiful. We were dead in our sins and He came to rescue us and forgive us and cleanse us from our unrighteousness.

I don't know what sin you are carrying around with you, but Jesus did not come into the world to condemn the world, but that the world might be saved through Him and have hope.

We have observed the moment in the life of the woman at the well and the life of Matthew when Jesus transformed them. Now, let's go beyond the moment of transformation to see how worship poured out of a beautiful life raised up from the ashes. Begin by reading John 12:1-8

Where was Jesus? (v. 1)

Who approached him? (v. 3)

Describe what Mary did? (v. 3)

What response did Mary get from Judas Iscariot? (v. 5)

What response did she get from Jesus? (v. 7-8)

The beauty Jesus created in Mary's life was expressed in her willingness to pour out her special treasure regardless of the reactions of those around her. Because of the great gift Jesus had given her and the change he brought to her life, she didn't think it was too much to give Him the most precious thing she had. She was surrendering something of great value because there was nothing more valuable to Mary than Jesus.

Consider for a moment who you would be and how different your life would be without Jesus' transforming power. Perhaps you would like to write a prayer of thanksgiving here to express your gratitude.

Now look at our key scripture and fill in the blanks below

"To console those who mourn in Zion, to give them _____ for _____, The oil of joy for mourning, the garment of praise for the spirit of heaviness; That they may be called _____ of _____, The _____ of the LORD, that He may be _____" (Isaiah 61:3 NKJV)

I surrender All

> *"Therefore, since we are surrounded by such a great cloud of witnesses, let us throw off everything that hinders and the sin that so easily entangles. And let us run with perseverance the race marked out for us, fixing our eyes on Jesus, the author and perfecter of faith. For the joy set before him he endured the cross, scorning its shame, and sat down at the right hand of the throne of God." ~ Hebrews 12:1-2*

I'm so thankful you've come with me for the final day of this study. We've seen the benefits of living a life surrendered to Jesus Christ. And yet, the question remains today, are you willing to surrender your life as a continual living sacrifice day after day, season after season, laying everything you are and everything that is most precious to you at His feet, trusting that if He asks you, then He has an eternal plan for His glory?

Remember, as we complete this study, surrender may not be easy. In my own life I've had times where surrender required total dependence on Him. These places of surrender destroy any thoughts of self-suffiency and taught me His grace "alone" is sufficient for me, His strength is made perfect in my weakness. Isn't your desire to live a life that will become a testimony of your love and faithfulness to Jesus Christ, who Himself laid it all down for you?

Turn with me to Genesis 17. Read verses 1-8.

How old was Abram and what did God say to him?

In Genesis 17:1, when God is confirming His covenant to Abraham, what name did God use for Himself in Genesis 17:1?

The Hebrew word El Shaddai means All Sufficient God - who is mighty in power and strength.

When God makes the covenant, He is mighty enough, sufficient enough, to keep the covenant. Abraham's job was to walk before him and be blameless.

Open to Genesis 22 and read verses 1-10.

What did God ask Abraham to do in verses 1-2.

What time of day did Abraham go? (v.3)

I'm trying to imagine Abraham waking up early and cutting wood, getting two servants, gathering Isaac from the house, and saddling the donkey, knowing full well what he was headed to do. According to verse 4, how many days passed before they saw their destination in the distance?

What did Abraham tell the servants in verse 5?

I think it's interesting that Abraham had enough faith to say, "We will worship and then we will come back to you." Describe verses 8-10.

Verse 9 says, Abraham bound his son Isaac and laid him on the alter on top of the wood. Isaac was old enough to struggle against what his father was doing, but instead he submitted to his father's will.

How can we relate? God had a clear plan with clear instructions for Abraham. Even though the instructions were clear, the instructions didn't seem to make sense. As you continue to live a life completely surrendered to God on a daily basis, He will instruct you clearly. You may not always fully understand the steps He places before you. Is there an area in your life that you have heard the Lord speak to you, but you are having a hard time understanding why this would be His way?

From the list below, circle the reasons for feeling this way? Please write any others that come to mind.

Past	Emotions	Desires	Current season	Own thoughts
Timing	Insecurities	Fears	Comfort zone	Other _____

Abraham demonstrated to all of us, faith requires steps of obedience even when we don't understand the "whys" behind our obedience.

Read Genesis 22:11-19.

What did God tell Abraham? (v. 12)

What did Abraham see? (v. 13)

What did he call the place? (v. 14)

What did the angel of the LORD tell Abraham? (vs.15-18)

We may be confused regarding how our steps of obedience will play out. But we can know one thing, God is faithful and He can be trusted on how this plays out.

At the end of verse 14 we hear, "And to this day it is said, 'On the mountain of the LORD it will be provided'" (see Genesis 22:14).

How can we know and trust God to provide for us? Because, what Abraham was experiencing was a foreshadowing of what God had planned before the foundation of the world. Jesus was the promised son, the first born over all creation. I know we can never fully grasp the cross from God's perspective, but let's read it fresh for ourselves.

Read Matthew 26:36-45

Describe how Jesus felt during this time in the garden?

What did Jesus say to the Father in verses 39 and 42?

Verse 46 begins with Jesus saying, "Rise, let us go!"

It was time! Jesus, "the image of the invisible God, the firstborn over all creation" (Colossians 1:15) was going to lay down His life for you and me. The night before the crucifixion He was taken before the High Priest to be judged. What does Matthew 26:65-68 say they did to Jesus?

Read Matthew 27:1-2. Let's describe the setting here. Time of Day:

Who was there?

What decision did they make?

Verse 2 tells us they bound him, led him away, and handed him over to Pilate, the governor. Read Matthew 27:11-26. Who told Pilate to crucify Jesus?

Before we go on, let's be reminded Jesus had willingly given Himself over to the Father's will. The time Jesus spent in the garden was of upmost importance, because He had to settle the matter in the garden. This is important, so when He gets to this point of physical, emotional, mental, and spiritual torment, with an external crowd, religious leaders, and now government leaders, crowding Him on all sides, He would not be moved.

Our Savior began His race with the end in mind. His crown, His victory was not silver or gold, but you and me. As you face your current struggle of surrender and testing of faith, know that Jesus also struggled through his obedience of faith when in the garden, even to the point of sweating blood. But when He was sure there was no other way, He arose from the garden and set His face like a flint to accomplish the work on the cross. You and I have to go forward with the end in mind, knowing that we can trust Jesus with what He is asking of us.

Read Luke 21:12-19 and write what stands out to you about what Jesus told the disciples.

Look at verse 19 in the margin and fill in the blanks below.

By standing firm you will gain life. Luke 21:19

"By _____ firm you will gain _____."

Now read 1 Corinthians 15:57-58 and fill in the blanks below

But thanks be to God! He gives us the _____ through our Lord Jesus Christ. Therefore, my dear brothers, _____ _____. Let nothing move you. Always give yourselves fully to the work of the Lord, because you know that your labor in the Lord is not in vain" (1 Corinthians 15:57-58).

Now continue reading Matthew 27:27-50.

From the perspective of the on-lookers Jesus' story at this point seemed to come to a tragic end. However, we know as 1 Peter 1:25 says, "but the word of the Lord endures forever." Jesus had accomplished everything the Father had willed Him to accomplish. His greatest work was on the cross. And the good news of the greatest surrender of all time would not be good at all if that was the end of the story of Jesus' life on earth. However, just as Jesus said He would, three days later, Jesus rose from the dead, three days later, showing Himself victorious over sin and death.

Go back to Genesis 22:9 and read what took place. Isaac was taken to the place God told Abraham about and the wood was arranged for the sacrifice. Isaac was placed on the wood. But God stopped the sacrifice and provided an alternative. But in Matthew 27, our Heavenly Father took His One and only Son, Jesus, and sacrificed Him for our sins. There was no other alternative for bringing salvation to men.

There has been no greater act of surrender in all of history than the surrender of the One who created all things. Jesus left His country, His home, and His Father and came to a world He created. He was born of a virgin in the humblest of circumstances, obediently confined himself to a body, and demonstrated God's love for us.

The day would come where he would pray to the Lord in the garden about the coming events. He then surrendered. Not His will, but God's be done. Jesus willingly laid down his life down on that cross, and took upon the sin of the whole world. He paid the ultimate price for you and me because He loves us. He surrendered all. You serve a Savior that not only surrendered everything for you, but lives to intercede for you. Ask yourself, am I willing to trust Jesus with all my life, including all my circumstances and decisions?

Today, LORD, I trust You with _____

_____

I, _____ (your name) will obey Your voice, trusting You to accomplish your will.

I think when all seems lost, God has a plan of redemption and when He shows up it is **forever**. And when that time comes, what does Revelation 21: 1-7 say?

"What, then, shall we say in response to this? If God is for us, who can be against us? He who did not spare his own Son, but gave Him up for us all – how will He not also, along with Him, graciously give us all things? Who will bring a charge against those whom God has chosen? It is God who justifies. Who is He that condemns? Christ Jesus, who died- more than that, who was raised to life – is at the right hand of God and is also interceding for us. Who shall separate us from the love of Christ? Shall trouble or hardship or persecution or famine or nakedness or danger or sword? As it is written: 'For your sake we face death all day long; we are considered as sheep to be slaughtered.' No, in all these things we are more than conquerors through Him who loved us" (Romans 8:31-37).

Look back at our key verse for today and fill in the blanks below.

"Therefore, since we are surrounded by such a great cloud of witnesses, let us _____

_____ everything that _____ and the sin that so _____ entangles. And let us

_____ with perseverance the race marked out for us, _____ our eyes on Jesus, the

_____ and _____ of faith. For the joy set before him he _____ the

cross, scorning its _____, and sat down at the right hand of the throne of God" (Hebrews 12:1-2).

I am grateful for your faithfulness in completing this study. I pray that you will look for opportunities in your life to surrender your will for the sake of God's glory. God bless you and keep you,

Regina

Notes

1. "Compassion." *Strong's Exhaustive Concordance: New American Standard Bible. 1995.* Updated ed. La Habra: Lockman Foundation. Accessed March 22, 2011. http://www.biblestudytools.com/concordances/strongs-exhaustive-concordance/.
2. "Distracted." Thayer, Joseph H., *Thayer's Greek-English Lexicon of the New Testament* (Hendrickson Publishers Peabody, MA, reprinted 2000).
3. "Good." HELPS Word-Studies -Biblos – Def 18 - Helps Ministries, Inc – http://strongsnumbers.con/greek/18.htm
4. Andrews, Andy. Butterfly Effect. Thomas Nelson Publishers, 2010. Print.

Special Thanks

I am so grateful to all those God has used to create and edit this study. I have learned an important lesson throughout this journey. We will not fulfill the calling God has on our lives without countless others walking with us. The writing may have started with one, but without the many others that came alongside in prayer, encouragement, support, and their own gifts of labor, knowledge, and wisdom, this study would have not been completed. I can say from the depths of my heart that God alone deserves any Glory that comes from the fruit of this study. As the psalmist said it best in Psalm 115:1, "Not to us, LORD, not to us, but to your name be the glory because of your love and faithfulness."

To Susan Lanier, who first picked up the rough draft and began editing, for all your prayers, phone calls, continuous editing, and help with the process of writing this Bible Study and for always pointing me to Jesus and continually reminding me His glory is the "one" purpose for this study.

To the ladies at First Baptist Church, Bainbridge GA, who participated in the original study of this word from God in its original, unedited form before I ever thought it would go any further than week five.

To my mom, Nancy, who spent countless hours helping edit and write day by day, week by week. Thank you for your continuous love and support.

To Chantal Orr, who also helped write and edit for countless hours. Thank you for all the graphics and ideas you have to make someone want to pick up the study. I heard it said, "You put music to words." I'll never forget the days spent at your house.

To Brenda, my friend, who gave me the first opportunity to teach the revised study with her Bible study group at First Baptist Church, Lone Oak, KY. Thank you for believing in this work, all your prayers, and hours of editing as well.

To all the ladies at Ledbetter Baptist, who also was a part of the first revised study. Thank you for your love and kindness.

To Ann Titsworth, who graciously took the cover photo and to Mrs. Bettie, Tera, and Maritess Melber, whose hands we see on the cover - three generations who have truly shown me what it means to surrender for God's glory - thank you also for your prayers.

To Martha Parker, I am so grateful for your support and prayers. Thank you for always believing in what God is doing in our lives and partnering with us throughout our journey. Without your support, we would not have made it this far. Thanks, also, for the help in editing.

To Tina, Kim, and all my friends who have prayed and encouraged me throughout the writing and editing of this study - I am so grateful for you all. Christy Lundy - thank you for the author photo.

To my children, Alexis, Bryce, Brianna, and Elijah – you are a joy and blessing to me.

To my husband Brian - besides the LORD Jesus, you are my best friend and there is no greater love in my life. You truly are an example of leadership and faith.

Printed in the United States
By Bookmasters